Don't Hire the Best

Photo courtesy Varun Madan

Abhijit Bhaduri works as the Chief Learning Officer for the Wipro group. He lives in Bangalore, India. Prior to this, he led HR teams at Microsoft, PepsiCo, Colgate and Tata Steel and worked in India, Southeast Asia and the US. He did his bachelor's degree with honours in economics from Shri Ram College of Commerce, Delhi University and then a post-graduation in human resources from Xavier Labour Relations Institute, Jamshedpur. He also has a degree in law from Delhi University.

He is on the advisory board of Wharton's prestigious programme for chief learning officers run by the University of Pennsylvania. He is an adviser on social media usage for Society of Human Resource Management (SHRM) in India and is among the top ten HR influencers on Social Media according to SHRM. He has written columns for the *Economic Times* and articles for the *Hindu Business Line*, *People Matters* magazine, and *Operations Research & Management Sciences Today*. He runs a popular blog at http://abhijitbhaduri.com

Abhijit has published two works of fiction with HarperCollins, India: *Married But Available* and *Mediocre But Arrogant*.

You can join him on Twitter at http://twitter.com/abhijitbhaduri, or email him at abhijitbhaduri@live.com

Advance Praise for *Don't Hire the Best*

'Hiring mistakes are expensive. At senior levels it is almost always about their fit with the organization's culture. This book tells you how to get it right. A very useful book for all involved in hiring high-potential talent.'

– Azim Premji, Chairman, Wipro Limited

'Abhijit Bhaduri's new book is a clearly written and well-informed discussion of the most important problem in business—how to find talented leaders. Based on the most recent research on the topic, the book argues that successful performance from a manager depends more on personality than education and experience. For those who believe in data-based solutions to crucial organizational problems, this book is for you.'

– Dr Robert Hogan, President, Hogan Assessments

'This is a must read for every person/corporate that wants to relook at the way hiring is done. The book not only provides interesting insights into the most obvious mistakes we make while hiring but also suggests some innovative solutions/insights to overcome them. Abhijit has made a convincing case, to *not* hire *the best*.'

– V.R. Ferose, Managing Director, SAP Labs India

'An insightful read about the importance of assessing the "whole" person while hiring people in leadership roles. If you are someone who makes hiring decisions, read this book before you hire the next person.'

– David Tessmann-Keys, SVP, International Operations,
Development Dimensions International Inc.

'Anyone building a business should read this book. Abhijit Bhaduri explains clearly and sympathetically why so many smart executives end up making foolish hiring decisions. Then he lays out a logical system that will help you escape such traps. His insights about sizing up candidates are both valuable and inspiring.'

– George Anders, winner of the Pulitzer Prize
and author of *The Rare Find*

Don't Hire the Best

An Essential Guide to Picking the Right Team

ABHIJIT BHADURI

HARPER
BUSINESS

First published in India in 2009 by Harper Element
An imprint of HarperCollins *Publishers*

Building No 10, Tower A, 4th Floor, DLF Cyber, City Phase II,
Gurugram 122002
www.harpercollins.co.in

This edition published in India in 2017 by Haper Business

P-ISBN: 978-93-5029-433-8
E-ISBN: 978-93-5029-551-9

6 8 10 9 7 5

Typeset in 11/14 Berthold Baskerville
Jojy Philip New Delhi 110 015

Printed and bound in India by
Replika Press Pvt. Ltd.

HarperCollins *Publishers*, Macken House, 39/40 Mayor Street Upper, Dublin 1, D01 C9W8, Ireland

To
Nandini, Eshna and Abhishek
Some hiring is best left to chance

Contents

Section 1

1

The Role of a Leader

INTRODUCTION

This book aims at helping you improve the way you hire people in leadership roles. I have used the term 'Leader' to mean the Chief Executive Officer (CEO) and his/her direct reportees. The ideas in this book would also be relevant while hiring someone whose role has a significant impact on the success or failure of an organization—a leader's role.

While every hiring is critical, at the senior level the stakes are high. Using the 80:20 ratio it is easy to say that the top 20 per cent leaders have 80 per cent impact on the organization. They impact business results, as also the quality of employees the firm can attract and retain. Above all they impact the culture of the organization. This book is about how to hire the leaders who will succeed.

We continue to use terms such as manager, CEO, leader, etc., just the way we have, over the last few decades, but the demands of those roles have changed drastically. Today's leaders need to handle rapidly changing legal and regulatory environments, a shifting consumer base, changing technology that affects the supply chain and work with an employee base that is technologically savvy and mobile.

What distinguishes the effective managers from the ineffective ones in a particular organization is known as the competency that a leader brings to his position.

Business leaders need four kinds of competencies (Hogan & Warrenfeltz, 2003):

Business Skills

These involve information processing. The person can do these by herself. Examples of business skills would be business acumen, strategic vision and decision making. Business skills involve planning, monitoring budgets, forecasting costs and revenues, cutting costs, mapping strategies, evaluating performance, running meetings and organizing necessary reports. These skills are the easiest to teach and depend on strong cognitive abilities. They can be done by a person in isolation unlike the three skills that follow. Since these business skills depend on cognitive ability rather than on interpersonal skill, many people believe that cognitive ability is important for managerial performance. To the degree that organizations select and evaluate managers on the basis of cognitive ability and business skills and ignore the other three competency domains; they ignore the human side of enterprise.

Leadership Skills

These are competencies needed to manage others. Examples of leadership skills would be building teams, delegation and managing performance. Leadership skills are all about building and maintaining effective teams. This has five components. The first is about the ability to recruit or attract talented people to form a team. The second involves retaining talented personnel after they have been recruited—and simply throwing money at people won't suffice. The third component of leadership skill is about the leader's ability to motivate a team—other things being equal, a motivated team will outperform a more talented but less motivated group. Recruiting, retaining and motivating team members depend on building positive relationships with each team member—a capability that vitally builds on the interpersonal skills developed earlier. The fourth component concerns developing, projecting and promoting a vision for the team. Projecting and promoting a vision is the core of charisma. The final component of leadership skill is about persistence and resilience.

Interpersonal Skills

Building trust, building relationships and influencing others are examples of these competencies. These skills help the leader to get along with others. People with strong interpersonal skills are poised, charming, approachable and rewarding to deal with. There are four elements of interpersonal skills—the ability to put oneself in another person's shoes, the ability to correctly anticipate another person's expectations, the ability to modify one's behaviour according to the other person's expectations and finally, having self-control to stay focused on the other person's needs.

Intrapersonal Skills

These refer to the self-regulatory competencies that are at the core of how a leader approaches the work assignment. These skills are developed based on the life experiences one has in the formative years. Intrapersonal skills have three components—self esteem, attitude towards authority and self control. People with strong self esteem are confident, are not easily frustrated or upset and do not have mood swings. They can quickly bounce back from setbacks. People with positive attitude towards authority follow rules, are conforming and easy to supervise. People with a high degree of self control find it easy to follow routines, are disciplined and can easily manage their impulses.

ASSESS WHAT CANNOT BE DEVELOPED

Not every gap in the new hire can be addressed by sending the person for a training programme or by assigning him a coach. Incidentally, fit with the role and the organizational culture is hard to develop. So look hard to assess a fit in these two areas.

The four competency clusters are all needed for anyone to perform a leadership role successfully. While hiring we always believe that if there is a shortfall in any of the competencies we can always bridge the gap through focused training and development efforts. But every competency is not equally developable. The intrapersonal competencies are especially hard to change. That explains why it is very hard for someone to learn to handle stress better. Ability to handle stress is an intrapersonal competency.

The intrapersonal competencies develop early in life followed by the development of interpersonal, leadership and business skills. The earlier a skill is developed the more difficult it is to change. So the important thing to remember is that while hiring it is far more important to assess intrapersonal and interpersonal skills than it is to assess the business ones.

Business skills such as the person's ability to take decisions under pressure can be assessed by interviewing the candidate or looking at the choices made by the person in earlier assignments. The ability to build teams and managing performance can only be assessed by doing a thorough reference check of the person. It is difficult to assess these only through an interview. Interpersonal and intrapersonal skills are hard to assess without using the right psychometric tools. Many of these are elements of personality that are not possible to be judged even by people who have been trained in interviewing techniques. People who are articulate and confident find it easy to answer these probes in interviews.

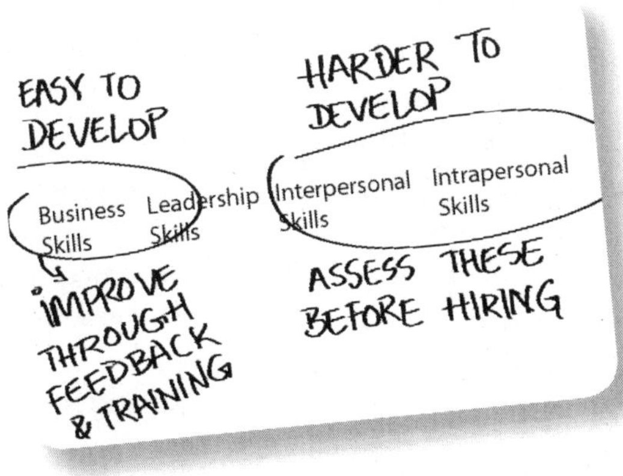

The demands of a job have a great bearing on the personality elements. Let us take two examples: An air traffic controller's job needs someone with a calm demeanour, low distractibility, high conscientiousness to be able to follow procedures to the letter and comfortable with routine. A salesperson on the other hand may need someone who is passionate about the product and possesses interpersonal skills, resilience and flexibility. So, in trying to understand what to look for in hiring a leader we need to know what the role is about.

In a leadership role, the person needs to be calm and stable, competitive and achievement oriented and friendly and agreeable. She should be conscientious and should follow rules, but should not be overly rigid or inflexible about rules and procedures. All hiring decisions have to be made keeping the role in mind. Personality elements that make a person successful in one role may actually turn out to be the reason why the person fails in a different one.

Exercise: Capability or Willingness

Most hiring dilemmas have to do with choosing between people who are all equally qualified to do the role. So the real differentiator is to find out which candidate will be motivated to do what the task demands without having to make a conscious effort.

Imagine having to choose from three equally qualified candidates—Alok, Bimal and Chirag. These are the three candidates who ran the operations of a heavy machinery manufacturer. Each one had worked for very reputed organizations. They impressed the interviewers with their business acumen and knowledge of the industry. Here is what happened to each one:

CANDIDATE 1: ALOK

Alok could set high goals for himself and his team. He was calm and confident. He crafted a great plan for the business that could put the company on a high growth path. But his peers found him very abrasive. They couldn't fault his logic but found his manner of communicating very hurtful even though what he said would be factually correct. Alok spent very little time in face-to-face meetings and preferred to send a weekly analysis to the organization about what they had done well and what was not up to the mark. He was fussy about details and a stickler for people following the rules that he had set and was known to brutally chastise anyone who did not comply. Alok left when he was repeatedly questioned about the dropping scores on employee engagement.

CANDIDATE 2: BIMAL

Bimal was a charismatic leader. He was self-assured and had offbeat and innovative ideas about how to run the business. He did not consult his peers and said none of them knew as much about marketing as he did. The risqué ad campaign that he launched left a lot of people in the leadership team very embarrassed. The campaign was written about extensively by the media as one showing poor taste. When asked if he saw this as a mistake, Bimal said that the ad had got more column centimetres of media space for the company in a month than what it got in a year. At the end of the launch conference, Bimal made some off-colour jokes about the lady who was interviewing him for a television channel. Bimal said in his defence that he was tired and had let down his guard.

He believed that the company will need to be far less traditional if it has to appeal to the new consumer segments. Bimal left within a month after the incident.

CANDIDATE 3: CHIRAG

Chirag had joined from a mid-sized company. He had crafted a compelling vision and was building a team that was highly engaged. He was developing a very confident second line by delegating tasks to this group while monitoring them closely. When one of his newly hired team members' spouse was hospitalized, Chirag made a recommendation to the Human Resources (HR) department to sanction a loan to him even though the person had not completed six months in the organization. Chirag made his displeasure known to everyone when the loan application was turned down. When the company shut down a loss-making unit, Chirag promised 'a generous' severance package to the affected employees. Before it was announced, he took the proposal to the CEO and asked for a substantial increase in the package. The CEO mentioned that Chirag was acting as the de facto union leader of the employees. When the 'revised' severance package was announced, Chirag went up to submit his resignation to a stunned CEO saying that he found it hard to work in a company which had no respect for human values. The CEO said that Chirag should work for an NGO where he can be truly altruistic.

Analyses

Alok's discomfort in social interactions is coming in the way of his role. He does not enjoy face-to-face interactions. His lack of diplomacy (even when he is factually correct) is alienating his colleagues. This personality element seems to be a barrier to his doing what the role demands. That affects his performance. He is not motivated to do a role that he is qualified to do. Lack of motivation will prevent Alok from succeeding in a leadership role. He will be a poor performer.

Bimal loves being the cynosure of all eyes. He would rather be controversial than ignored. This personality characteristic is proving to be very expensive to the organization. His behaviour when under stress is proving to be a liability for the organization. This personality element is proving to be a derailer that is coming in the way of someone who is otherwise qualified to do the role and also affecting his performance in the role and his image as a leader.

Chirag is a great example of a leader leaving because of a mismatch between his values and the organization's. The organization's culture is the context in which a role is performed. If there is a low fit between the individual and the organization, the person may not be fully engaged, and it will eventually lead to the person leaving the organization. Attrition at the senior level is usually indicative of a mismatch between the values of the person involved and the organization. The better the fit, the more satisfied a person will be.

To find out which of the three candidates should have been hired, we need to understand not just the demands of the role, but also the culture of the organization. Alok is not motivated to succeed. He will always underperform. Bimal may achieve the targets but will always behave in a manner that will be controversial. In an organization culture that is conservative, which may be a challenge in a paternalistic and traditional organizational culture,

Chirag's behaviour will be highly popular—at least among the employees but may not be viewed with as much indulgence by the board especially during times of recession.

IDEAS

1. Everyone who is qualified to do a role may not be able to do the role. While in the short run people may stretch themselves and demonstrate the appropriate behaviour needed for the role, eventually their performance will drop because they do not have the personality elements that are 'enablers'. Enabling elements in one's personality help the person to succeed in doing what one is qualified to do. A proper fit between the person and the role is an important predictor of performance.
2. People have some behaviours that can be derailers in a leadership role. Strengths when overused become derailers. For example, getting into details may be seen as a strength in a middle management role. In a leadership role, the same behaviour will be seen as micro managing. This can impede performance. Derailing behaviours can lead to the downfall of leaders who are otherwise high performers.
3. A motivational fit with the role helps a person succeed. Job satisfaction is driven by a fit between the individual's and the organization's values. We shall explore in a later chapter of this book how to assess individual values, motivations and preferences. This can be an important predictor of employee engagement, and a low fit will lead to attrition of high-performing and otherwise successful employees.

2

Hiring 'The Best'

Organizations hire people every day. There are vacancies at various levels. These vacancies have to be filled. People have to be promoted to take up bigger assignments. Citizens have to 'hire' the politicians who will represent them. At home we need to hire domestic help. We hire doctors and lawyers. Parents have to hire tutors. Even the mafia don has to hire team members and bodyguards. A wrong hiring of a bodyguard could make all the difference between life and death. So hiring the right person is a critical task. Entrepreneurs soon discover that it is not enough to have a business plan; they need the right leaders to grow the business.

Leadership is a complex process. So it is natural that it is tempting for the organization to find the best person in leadership roles.

They can either hire 'the best' or they can hire the right person. When we hire someone because she has the best qualifications (usually from prestigious colleges and institutions) and has worked in one or more of the best-known organizations, we believe we are hiring 'the best'.

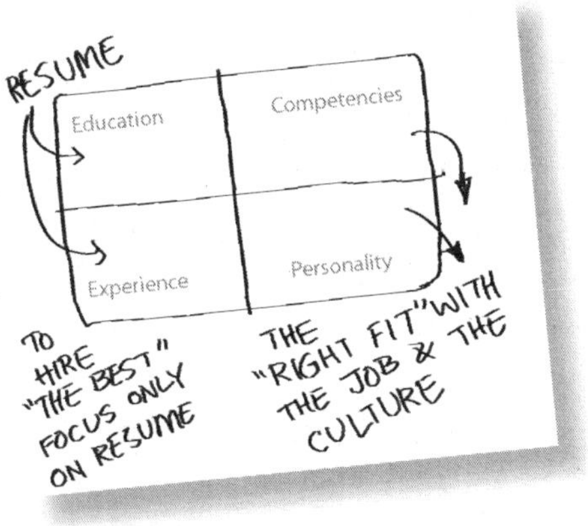

Research clearly shows that at leadership levels, success is determined more by personality fit than qualifications and experience.

Arount 95 per cent of hirings happen by focusing on the left side of the diagram i.c., what is written in a resume. A few firms assess competencies. Competencies are the 'what and how' of the role. What does this person need to do in the role to be successful? Is the person motivated to do what she is eminently qualified to do? This is where assessing the personality of the candidate can make a difference. For that we need the right instrument and have the results interpreted by people who are trained in that instrument. When we focus on hiring people based on assessment of competencies and personality, it is the 'Right Hire' (these two blocks are also on the right side!).

Assessing personality is a specialized task. It is hard to imagine doing all that for every entry-level job. My suggestion is that you use the 'Right Hire' approach while hiring the top team. Do not hire the best at the top.

When asked why is hiring the right person so hard and why do we get it wrong so often, the author of *The Rare Find*, Pulitzer Prize winning author George Anders says in an interview (Bhaduri, 2012):

> Good hiring shouldn't be difficult—but human nature often tugs leaders and hiring managers in the wrong direction. The most common error is to look for candidates who sound impressive in the interview room, without making much of an effort to gauge the actual skills, motivation and character traits necessary to be successful on the job. Whether it's in the United States or India, there's a tendency to favour people who are smooth conversationalists, confident and neatly presented. There's nothing wrong with those traits—but they aren't the main event. To wit:
>
> In technical fields, socially awkward people with great domain expertise and great motivation get short-changed. They don't make it past early screening, in favour of someone who seems much more polished but may not be nearly as hard-working or savvy.
>
> In sales jobs, you need to make sure that you are hiring someone who will be willing to do the hard work to sell *your* product—not someone whose greatest skill is selling himself or herself. This is a blunder that gets repeated somewhere in the world almost every time that a second hand ticks forward on a watch. Companies keep hiring supposed sales stars who don't really want to do the hard work of learning the territory; treating customers well, getting up to speed on the products, building teams, etc.
>
> In general management, team-building skills (or lack of them) can be completely overlooked. Great leaders are firm but fair. They rally subordinates, customers,

regulators, etc., to their point of view without using more force than necessary. A careful look at someone's work history and references can establish who is good at this and who isn't. In a social interview, though, it's much harder to tell. That's why companies end up hiring the infamous 'leaders without any followers.'

WHY SHOULD YOU 'HIRE RIGHT'?

Talent is necessary for leaders to succeed, but if they are not intrinsically motivated to succeed, having talent does not yield great performance. For thirty-five years, researchers have been exploring how motivation affects creativity. In studies involving groups as diverse as children, college students, professional artists and knowledge workers, we have found that people are more creative when they are more strongly intrinsically motivated—driven by interest, enjoyment, satisfaction and a sense of personal challenge in the work they are doing. (Amabile & Kramer, 2012)

Hiring right involves understanding many hidden aspects:

What Personality Factors will Help the Person Succeed: When a new hire takes up a role, the person needs to have a fit with the role. Defining the success factors of the role is a good place to initiate the hiring process. What behaviours will enable the person to succeed in the role? This role-person fit determines how well the person will do the role. There are elements of personality that will help the person do the role well. These are enablers. For instance, the ability to see the big picture could be an enabler in several senior-level roles. Assessment of the 'Bright Side' of the personality tells us if the person is able

to do what the role needs him to do. This is how others will see the person on a day-to-day basis. If you are asked what someone is like, chances are that you are describing what the person's bright side is like.

What Personality Factors will Derail the Person: The 'dark side' of the personality (see the diagram above) tell us about the derailers that will crop up when the person is not actively managing his or her public image. These risks emerge when the person's guard is down because of stress or when the person is extremely tired. It may happen even when the person is extremely comfortable in the presence of the people who are around him. The bright and dark side of the personality together tell us the extent of the fit of the person and the role.

What Motivates the Person: The fit between the person and the role also involves assessing what the person values most in a job or career and an organization. Besides checking for a person–role fit, the right hire will be one who fits well with the organization's culture. The role of Chief Financial Officer (CFO) in a large global software company will be very different from that of the CFO in a financial institution. The skills required to be successful as a CFO in an entrepreneurial start-up will be different. The fit for this lies in matching the values of the person with the culture of the organization.

I have deliberately limited the focus on using the right-hire approach while hiring the top leaders because the impact of a single wrong hire at the top is huge. Use this approach for others as well if you like. If you think that it takes too much effort, at least use it while hiring your top leaders.

In order to understand how hiring is done in different organizations and for different roles I spoke to a number of friends and fellow human resources (HR) professionals. For the past few years I have been studying what makes for successful hiring at the top. I learnt about how airlines hire pilots, how hospitals hire doctors, how the army hires its officers and how hotels hire housekeepers. I discovered many interesting approaches that employers have devised to hire the right person.

For instance, one of the largest hotel chains across the world told me how they show two almost identical photos of a freshly made room to applicants for their housekeeping job. One of the photos has a slight wrinkle on the sheet. The amount of time it takes for a person to spot that is a good predictor of success in a housekeeping role.

I have spoken to several heads of HR and top search firms that specialize in hiring at the leadership level. I have studied cases of successful hiring and drawn upon my own experience of hiring and working with leaders in the different sectors and countries I have had a chance to work in. Many of those cases have been mentioned in this book. I have changed the identity (and occasionally even the gender) of the persons and the organizations, but the incidents are real.

Right hire at the leadership level involves knowing the requirements of the role that you are hiring for. Defining this is the first step. Beyond this you have to define the behaviours and personality elements that will be needed to be successful in the role.

IDEAS

1. Hiring 'the best' means hiring a person based on what is written in their resume. It is easy to believe that someone who has studied in top institutions and worked in world-class companies should be hired. At leadership levels, the education and previous work experience have limited impact. It is the personality of the candidate that creates a fit between the role and the culture of the organization. The 'right hire' is one who has the best fit.

2. There are four elements to be evaluated while making a hiring decision. (a) Education: Does the person have the necessary education or certification that equips him with the academic knowledge and licenses that are required to do the role? (b) Experience: During the course of his employment with other organizations, has the leader gathered the experience that will help him to deliver what the role expects him to? (c) Competencies: How does the leader differentiate himself and with what level of proficiency while doing the task? (d) Personality: What are the elements of personality that will enable him to do the role and what derailers could come in the way? Is there a good fit between the role, the organizational culture and the individual?

3. Education and experience work well at entry level roles. At leadership levels, the personality affects the performance very strongly. Personality elements need to be studied through psychometric assessments. Trained interviewers can grade a candidate on what he can do and how he does it. But it takes someone trained to be able to use the appropriate psychometric instrument to understand why a person does what he does.

3

What I Learnt and How

When I was a student of HR at Xavier Labour Relations Institute (XLRI), Jamshedpur, there were courses that I took on recruitment and selection. It did not seem very complicated. I declared myself ready to start interviewing and hiring people. It so happened that when I joined the corporate sector, in the very first year at work, I was sent to hire fresh engineers from the colleges across the country. It would be a team of two looking more like travelling salesmen, who would visit colleges trying to find people who would not be rejected when they would go for their final round of interviews with the hiring team in our head office. I suddenly realized that it was I and not the candidate who was having performance anxiety.

> note to myself LESSON #1
>
> questions in the interview are not about stumping the candidate,
>
> LOOK FOR 'ROLE-FIT' & "CULTURE FIT" IN THE ANSWERS

My colleague would grill them on their subject knowledge and then hand them over to me to find a suitable fit of the candidate and the organizational culture. On seeing how I was going about the task, my colleague assured me that what I asked them did not matter since their domain knowledge was assured. Knowing that I could not do any damage I went about my task trying to see what question could possibly yield the insights that would help me decide. *My first lesson in hiring was that it did not matter what questions I asked.* The skill lay in decoding what the candidate said and to judge whether the person would be a good fit for the role they were being chosen for.

I continued my journey as an HR person through different companies and sectors of Corporate India from Tata Steel, Mudra, Colgate, PepsiCo, Microsoft and Wipro. I handled hiring of candidates from blue-collar workers to campus hires and more at the leadership level. That led to the insight that forms the core message of this book. Successful hiring needs four elements to be looked at. These are: (a) Education; (b) Experience; (c) Competencies and (d) Personality.

These four elements define success for a role. So this is called a Success Profile℠—a term used by Development Dimensions International, popularly known as DDI (http://www.ddiworld.com). They specialize in assessing and developing leaders.

I am a big believer in the value of creating a Success Profile℠ when it comes to hiring at the leadership level. Before you start hiring a leader, ask yourself what elements in each of these boxes will be necessary to make the person successful. Just identify the key elements of each factor. Think of people who have performed that role. What made them succeed? That is what you need to add for each of the four factors of a Success Profile℠.

Education

Education refer to the academic degrees and certifications that are needed to do the job. So to perform a role involving designing a machine you need a person to have a degree in mechanical engineering. Simply put, this tells us the knowledge required to do the job.

Experience

Like qualifications, a person's experience is also articulated well in his resume. What kind of organizations and projects has the person had an opportunity to apply his knowledge to? How often have they applied his knowledge and in what kind of varying circumstances is assessed by analysing the work experience of the candidate. When one is looking to hire someone directly from the campus, the person would have qualifications but no experience. Almost all hiring decisions tend to use these two boxes extensively. While hiring an experienced person you need to specify the *kind of experience* that the job demands. What about hiring someone who has managed a large team of inexperienced but qualified accountants in multiple countries? Are you looking for someone who has launched luxury soaps in Africa? Would it be better to look for someone with ten years of general management experience in a family-run business managing several factories and branches in India or do you want someone with ten years of experience in a global multinational having worked in at least three different countries? The nuances of work experience should be articulated.

Competencies

A handful of hiring decisions are also influenced by measuring candidates on their competencies. Competencies tell us the behaviour a person needs to show while accomplishing the task. Two different roles may need varying proficiency levels of the same competency. If a

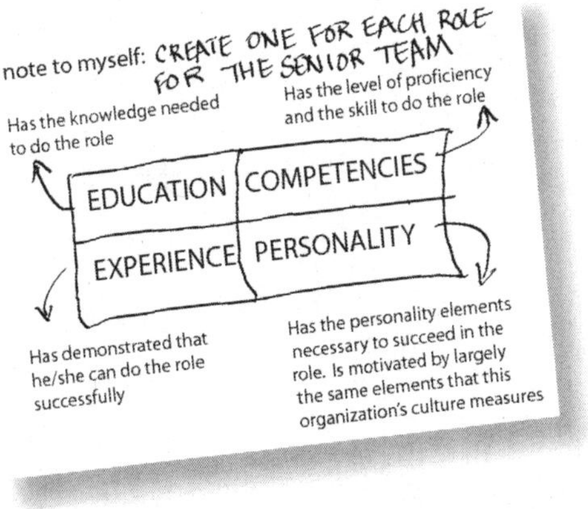

leader is going to work with an inexperienced team, the role will need someone strong in coaching and mentoring. So the kind of behaviour we may need to see is the person's ability to ask questions to gain understanding, help others think through issues or processes, or help others find their own answers. Competencies tell us what the candidate needs to do in the role. The hiring process can measure the proficiency level of every competency. What it does not measure is how a person does it or why a person does not do it well.

Personality

The missing piece of the jigsaw puzzle is assessing personality to understand the fit of the person to the role and the organization. If a certain element of personality, for example, social skill, tact, or perceptiveness are high, the person will seem to be friendly, warm and popular. This could be indicative of the person's interpersonal

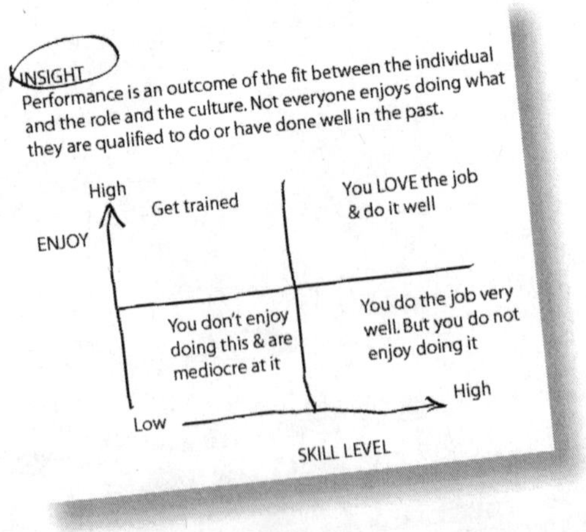

sensitivity. Low scorers will seem independent, frank and direct. A person who likes to be with people and is highly gregarious, (let us call it 'sociability') will be someone who is outgoing and will dislike working alone. Someone who is low on interpersonal sensitivity will seem reserved and quiet; she would avoid calling attention to herself and would not mind working alone. So, if coaching and mentoring is an important element of the role, it is best to not have someone who is low on sociability and interpersonal sensitivity. When a role matches the personality of the person, the person does the role well. Successful people stay longer in a role than unsuccessful ones. They do not need to quit because of performance issues. It is no wonder that so many mentorship programmes in companies never take off. They are simply assigned to people based on the requirement of a role without any sense of what the personality of the person is.

As I started to hire people in leadership roles I had my second insight on hiring. *The measurement of personality is*

the greatest predictor of fit with the role and the culture. The role operates in the context of the organization's culture. This ensures that the person does what the role demands and does it well. The assumption is that, if they match, the person will perform well and hence stay long enough in the role. The motives and values of the candidate have to fit with the organization's values for the person to be successful. This ensures that the organization provides the person what he or she needs to feel engaged. This fit ensures that the person is highly engaged in the organization.

CASE

Neera joined as the head of marketing of a very reputed consumer goods company. The company has been very successful in the past with its washing powder formulation. Their luxury soap for women was seen by many to be superior to their competitor's as far as the technical specifications were concerned. The soap had received lukewarm response in the market which surprised the CEO who was also the owner. The owner himself had been closely involved in the formulation and in the initial launch. A week after Neera had joined, a salesman asked her about the future of the soap during the annual meeting of all employees. Neera said that the soap had been launched without adequate market research and the chances of success were slim. Everyone held their breath because they knew that the CEO himself had supervised the research findings. But to everyone's surprise, the CEO applauded Neera for her candour and appreciated his grasp of the market dynamics. The response to Neera's remarks is a reflection of the fit with the culture of the organization and value of being candid. In another organization, the same behaviour might have evoked a different response. By the way, Neera had completed fifteen very successful years in that company when we last spoke.

Analysis

The individual and organizational values, when matched, will result in the employee being highly engaged. Organizational citizenship is an outcome of the extent of match between the values fit with the person and the company—at least with the key stakeholder(s). So if the personality has such a great influence on hiring success how do we ensure this happens? It is difficult for most people to assess personality or motivational fit by asking questions. Why, you may ask. That is because it is not about asking questions. It is about decoding the response to see if that gives us a view of a fit with the role and the organizational culture. It is best done by using psychometric instruments designed to assess these elements. Every psychometric instrument cannot do that either. I am going to talk about Hogan Assessments in great detail and why I believe that they provide the assessment of different elements of personality that are the right predictors of success in hiring (http://www.hoganassessments.com/).

Over the years I had a third 'aha' moment. When I started interviewing people I believed that there are some traits that are universally desirable in every job and in every organization. Taking initiatives and being creative was always seen as desirable by me. I learnt this lesson the hard way too. In some jobs like that of an auditor or for someone in charge of security, it could be a derailer. Note to me: *All personality elements, 'derailers', motivation and values have to be seen in the context of the role for which we are hiring.*

The degree to which the candidate fits the needs of a job or an organization will dictate success or failure.

A person who is successful as a salesperson will possess an outgoing, relationship-building interpersonal style. He may be high on risk taking. All these are elements that can be measured in the personality profile. By contrast someone being hired to be an air traffic controller needs to be even tempered, conscientious and not have a high need for social interactions to avoid being distracted on the job. Hiring someone with an outgoing, risk-taking personality may be the wrong personality fit in the air traffic controller's job. Without assessing the personality of two identically qualified people, we could make a choice that may be disastrous.

But even before you start assessing personality, you have to create a Success Profile^{SM} of the role. This book is all about the secret sauce of hiring the right senior leaders. Certainly do not hire the best at the top.

IDEAS

1. People who make better hiring decisions do so because they know what the candidate's answers reveal about the person's values and motives. In case the interviewer is looking to assess a competency, it is important to look for a real situation when a candidate can tell you what she actually did in that scenario rather than what she would/should do. Past behaviour is a good predictor of future behaviour. If you are trying to assess the person's planning skill, ask her to describe a scenario when she had to actually plan for a project. How did she go about estimating the timelines and tasks? What did she get right and how did she fix things when they did not go as per schedule?

2. The measurement of personality is the greatest predictor of fit with the role and the culture. That can help avert attrition at the leadership level. That alone might be a strong reason for you to do it. At senior levels, the differentiator of two equally competent leaders is personality. Measure whether the candidate's personality will enable or come in the way of doing the task. Measuring personality will help you match the motivators and values of the candidate with the organization's culture.

3. A personality factor that may be a strength in one role might be a liability in another. Strength, if overused, can be a derailer. Ask if that personality element will enable the person to be successful, or would it be a barrier. The value fit between the individual and the organization can impact the satisfaction level of the leader. Low fit results in the leader quitting the role or the organization even when he has a successful track record of performance.

4

Boss, What's the Secret Sauce?

Imagine answering these questions in an interview:

'Name five uses of a stapler without staple pins.'

'If you could be a superhero, what power would you possess?'

'In how many different ways can you get water from a lake at the foot of a mountain to its top?'

'Given twenty "destructible" light bulbs (which break at a certain height) and a building with a hundred floors, how do you determine the height at which the light bulbs break?'

'If you were a Microsoft Office programme, which one would you be?'

These are a small sample of questions that were actually asked to screen candidates in interviews. Every now and then we hear of the unique ways in which companies around the world try to find the right person to join the top team. Asking candidates to answer some of these questions is one of the methods. Some ask the candidates to solve puzzles. Some employers will invite a candidate to a restaurant or bar and then observe how the person behaves while waiting for others to show up. There are stories about a CEO who hires his team by taking a prospective candidate to play golf.

There are CEOs who swear that they hire based on their gut reaction. Then there are companies that have detailed interviews that run into twenty to thirty rounds before they hire someone. There are companies like Google whose hiring method has spawned thousands of posts on the net and several books because Google receives a million job applications a year and hires only one of every 130 people interviewed.

Hiring is complex. We may hire the wrong person and worse still we may actually reject the right candidate. Twelve publishers are said to have rejected J.K. Rowling's manuscript of *Harry Potter* that went on to sell 400 million copies and made Rowling richer than the Queen of England. This is a perfect example of rejecting the right candidate!

I am sure you have your share of stories about unusual questions that were asked in an interview or about an answer that stumped the interview panel. There is a certain mystique about the hiring process especially since most people who make hiring decisions have never been trained in interviewing skills. So everyone follows his own recipe. The result is that the outcome is entirely left to chance.

IT MATTERS MORE AT THE SENIOR LEVEL

I have chosen to focus on senior level hiring in this book and by that I mean the CEO and the roles that report to the CEO. The references are gender neutral even though I am using the masculine gender in the text.

All ideas and examples in this book will be limited to improving hiring decisions at this level. Hiring right at this level matters as much for a large corporation as it does for a start-up. Stakes are higher for candidates who are being screened for top jobs in a corporation. The successful candidates are going to be paid a huge sign-on bonus. That is just for starters. They will be the ones who will be paid the big bucks and fancy perks. They will be introduced to the media and showered with attention. At senior levels the new hires will come in and change many existing practices and team members and bring in their insights and even quirks into the new workplace. All the disruption is worth it if the new hire gets results, makes the company more successful and stays long enough in the company to build a team and leave a legacy. Organizations with effective hiring systems rank higher in financial performance, productivity, quality, customer satisfaction, employee satisfaction and retention.

Every company will have its own share of horror stories of wrong hires made at the very top. These hiring disasters leave behind a wreckage of lost business, infuriated customers and a devastated team. The price of a wrong hire is sometimes irreversible. Failure of senior leaders is never attributed to their lack of adequate experience or their not having the right qualifications for the role.

Why is it so important to assess personality of a candidate for a top job? The more senior the person is in an organization, the less are the checks and balances for that person. So personality factors assume tremendous importance. The CEO's personality whether in a small entrepreneurial set-up or in a large firm has a huge influence on the culture of the firm. The CEO can create processes and systems that reflect his own needs. If anyone else at the middle-management level were to bring in those very changes, it would be limited to a part of the organization. The personality of the senior leaders has an extraordinary effect on the organization's culture. So make sure you assess it using a psychometric instrument designed to measure personality elements that are relevant to the role and organizational fit.

At senior levels personality can make all the difference between two candidates who are both equally qualified for the role. If at the senior level the hiring processes are no different from the approach taken to hire someone at the junior or middle level we may be moving towards making a hiring error.

If we need a new CEO to turn an organization around, we tend to focus on someone who has had a successful experience of doing this. The board of many a company has had to step in and fire a CEO who was otherwise extremely competent and had an enviable track record. Psychologists often refer to 'Personality Derailers' that can often destroy an otherwise brilliant professional.

A leader may find it difficult to stay composed under pressure and this single behaviour may lead to his behaving in a manner that is inappropriate. We have all seen examples of someone who has sharp analytical skills but is unable to succeed in a role that requires a high degree of tact and the ability to handle a diverse team.

WHY NOT HIRE A STAR?

When a senior leader joins an organization, the fit with the role and the organization's culture can lead to the person's failure far more sharply than the qualifications or even success in the previous work experience. This is fairly counter-intuitive. If you have to hire someone from outside the company, why settle for a 'B' player? In a study called 'The Risky Business of Hiring Stars' documented in the May 2004 issue of *Harvard Business Review* they captured this sentiment accurately:

> 'Only the pick of the class can cope with today's business world, where executives have to anticipate change, adapt quickly and make decisions amid uncertainty, right? Besides, A players are ambitious, brainy, dynamic—and charismatic. When you recruit talent from outside the organization, which is inevitable since developing people within the firm takes time and money, why settle for B players? Hitch your wagon to a rising star and the company's profits will soar.'

The article goes on to say that most of stars fail in their new organizations despite their successful track record with the previous employer. The procedure, personalities, relationships and subcultures usually prove to be far more complex to master for these stars and this leads to abject failure in most cases. The stars don't stay very long in the new firm either, the study shows. 'Around 36 per cent of the stock analysts left the investment banks that hired them within 36 months and another 29 per cent quit in the next 24 months.'

RIGHT HIRE WRONG COMPANY

We are all familiar with stories of highly qualified stars hired from certain marquee companies to repair an ailing company, only to fail and cost the company dearly in the process. Robert Nardelli was brought in from GE to lead Home Depot. His operating style that had made him ever so successful in GE was a disaster at Home Depot. He was replaced but not before considerable damage was done to the business, the employees and the shareholders.

Leo Apotheker was named CEO of Hewlett-Packard on 30 September 2010. Apotheker, then fifty-seven, was a native German who had spent two decades with business software vendor SAP before ascending to the top job of SAP in April 2008. HP pointed to Apotheker's international experience as one of the reasons for the hire. The press release described him as a strategic thinker with a passion for technology, wide-reaching global experience and proven operational discipline. His strong points were his creativity and skill as a salesman. He was out of HP less than a year later, blamed for a downturn in the company's financial performance. He lasted only for ten months as the CEO at SAP; at HP he was there for eleven months.

While businesses have become more complex, the board's patience with CEOs has become more tenuous. No wonder that the tenure of CEOs have shortened over the past ten years. Overall, CEO tenures were on an average eighteen months shorter in 2010 (6.6 years) compared to a decade ago (8.1 years). And the length of planned tenures, in which the CEO departs on a date prearranged in agreement with the board, has dropped by 30 per cent over the last ten years, from ten to seven years. Of would-be CEO successors hired externally, 75 per cent don't become chief executives, or, if they do, they don't last for more than two years.

Year 2011 was the twelfth consecutive year that Booz & Company has been following the fortunes of CEOs at the world's 2,500 largest public companies; 14.2 per cent of those CEOs have been replaced. Although that rate is sharply higher than the previous year's turnover rate of 11.6 per cent, it essentially represents a return to the seven-year historical average of just over 14 per cent and it is one percentage point higher than the overall twelve-year average of 13.2 per cent. In 2011, the CEO turnover rate was highest among the 250 largest companies, as it has been, for the most part, since 2005. This trend has also been true over the past twelve years.

While the study points to the complexity of running large companies as the possible reason for the high turnover, I believe that it is more because of the lack of fit between the personality of the CEO, the demands of the role and the ability of the leader to operate within the ambit of the company culture. CEOs hired from outside the company were almost twice as likely to be forced out, over the last three years, as those elevated from within, according to the study. (Favaro, Karlsson, & Neilson, 2012)

The personality fit of the CEO with the organization's culture is a significant factor for success at the top. Here is the point I want you to think about. Each of these CEOs was selected because the board or the decision makers felt that the candidate they were betting on was the best choice. Interestingly, no one has heard of a CEO being asked to go because he did not have the right qualifications (though inaccuracies on Yahoo CEO Scott Thompson's resume have been the reason he stepped down in May 2012) or work experience. The reason for success or failure in leadership roles is always about behaviour that is linked to personality elements. Let us discuss this aspect a little more.

PERSONALITY: IDENTITY OR REPUTATION

Personality should be defined from two perspectives. First, there is the personality as we see it from inside, which is called identity. This is the person you think you are and it is best defined by your hopes, dreams, aspirations, goals and intentions; that is, your values. To find a fit between the organization's culture and the candidate, we need to measure the candidate's values and motivations.

Second, there is the personality from outside, which is called reputation. This is the person that others think you are and is best defined in terms of self-confidence, sociability, integrity, charm and creativity, or their opposites. Measuring a person's reputation can be a good predictor of fit between the person and the role. A person's reputation is the way most people will view the leader. So if we can measure it before we decide to hire the person, we can take a more informed decision. A sales leader needs to demonstrate energy, social skills and the ability to solve problems for customers. A candidate who does not demonstrate this will not be a good fit in a sales role.

There are often important disparities between a person's identity and his/her reputation and the size of the disparity is related to career success. The difference between how an individual sees himself and the reputation that he carries can be interesting to see. A leader may take pride in his ability to get into details. This skill is highly valued in the middle level since the reportees are relatively inexperienced. In a senior leadership role with experienced reportees, the same behaviour of the leader checking every presentation slide by slide may give the leader a reputation of being a micro manager. The term detail oriented or micro manager is then a matter of perception. It depends on the person from whose point of view we are describing the behaviour. This is illustrated in the following case study.

CASE

> Emraan was the head of marketing for a large cement manufacturer. He took pride in his ability to delve deep into the work of his team. He would call for frequent meetings and ask his team members to show him the working documents for every proposal. He would go over each step of their plan and told his direct reportees that they could call him at any time on his mobile if they needed his support or if they simply wanted to bounce an idea off him. When asked he would describe himself as someone who liked to get his hands dirty and detail-oriented. He lost four of his direct reportees in the span of a month. In the exit interviews they all spoke about Emraan's style being extremely suffocating. They resented his micro managing their work. They spoke about lack of work-life balance because they were spending long hours in meetings with Emraan every day. When the head of HR shared the comments made by his reportees during the exit interview Emraan said that he definitely did not micro manage anyone but that he liked to get into the details.

Organizations battle with the twin problems of high attrition and low employability. Indian organizations struggle to manage high turnover among employees.

They manage attrition by throwing money at the problem. While the employee may get a salary hike when they join a new employer, very rarely, the trigger to quit is monetary compulsion. Some attribute employee turnover to 'too much money chasing too few employable people.' The answer may lie elsewhere. High turnover among employees may well be because of poor hiring decisions that lead to a mismatch between the personality of the employee and the requirements of the role or the culture of the organization.

The Conference Board is a non-profit, non-partisan business membership and research group. Their publication called *Sleepless in Delhi* (June 2011) says: India's shortage of job-ready talent creates a seller's market. In 2010, turnover averaged 30 per cent across industries, ranging from 13 per cent in manufacturing to 35 per cent in financial and other services.

A successful hire at the leadership level should result in lowered attrition across the organization and a rise in the employee engagement. Engagement is largely a function of how someone is treated at work by their leaders. If the employee's psychological needs are met at work, he or she gets psychologically engaged. A good match between the employee's and employer values could be the answer to solving the attrition problem. To solve the problems of attrition and low employee engagement, take a close look at your hiring practices.

LEADERSHIP STYLE AFFECTS BUSINESS RESULTS

I thought of asking The Hay Group (http://www.haygroup.com/in/) what their research shows. The answer is clear.

Their research shows that business performance improves when the job requirements are matched by the individual motives and competencies and by working with a leader whose leadership style is aligned to the organizational climate. This results in significantly higher business performance than what would happen if any of the following factors was missing:

1. **Individual Competencies** tell us why you do what you do,
2. **Job Requirements** tell us what is required to be done,
3. **Managerial Style** impacts how we do a task and
4. **Organizational Climate** is the net effect on the organization.

Better climate leads to more discretionary effort by the employee. This is often referred to as employee engagement. In other words, when there is a match between the individual competencies, the job, the leadership style and the right organizational climate, that kind of an environment produces 30 per cent more output. It motivates the people to go above and beyond what they are meant to deliver. Almost 70 per cent of the organizational climate is affected by the leadership style. We all seem to instinctively understand that a great leader can motivate us to give our best. A bad leader can have a negative impact on the organizational climate, that is, the way people feel about working in that organization. Leaders who can tailor their behaviour, or leadership styles, to a situation create positive climates. Good working environments—or climates—energize and focus people to do their best. Mediocre climates dampen motivation and diminish performance. Of all the things that influence climate, the leaders have the greatest impact. So it is important to choose the right leader who can create a winning climate. This is reproduced in the following diagram reproduced from The Hay Group with permission.

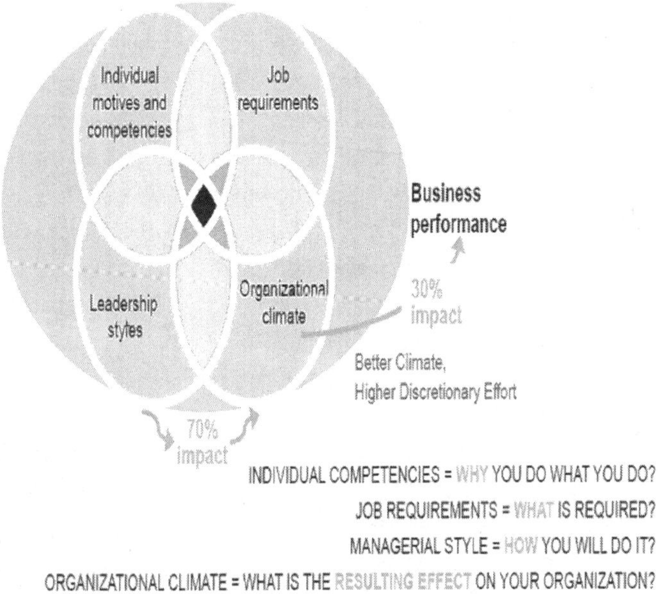

THE SECRET SAUCE: PERSON, ROLE AND CULTURE FIT

What we need to look for in hiring an experienced leader is very different from the time and resources an organization will spend in hiring at the junior or middle level. At the junior or middle level, the success of a new hire depends on the qualifications and quality of previous work experience. While hiring a senior leader the emphasis has to be on finding a fit between the person, the role and the organization's culture. This is amply demonstrated in the following case:

CASE

When Freida took over the reins of the sales team of a highly successful family-run auto ancillary, she had the reputation of being a rainmaker. She had single handedly grown her previous employer's business, a small family-owned advertising and public relations firm to become a media powerhouse. With her previous employer Freida had grown the business by 40 per cent year on year, even in difficult years. She worked her magic even at the new organization and quickly expanded the distribution network. She launched the new sales incentive system at a glitzy function in a five-star hotel with a TV star playing host. At the end of the function, Freida announced a trip to the Far East for the sales team, who were on a high having exceeded their annual sales targets. The family members were livid. Freida was asked to leave.

The patriarch of the family told me, 'She (Freida) had brought in a 'flashy five-star culture' that is at odds with our understated and frugal culture. People are paid to work hard and achieve targets. This is the typical ad agency mentality of partying at the drop of a hat. The sales team has earned huge bonuses and incentives for beating the targets. First it is this function being held at a five-star hotel followed by a foreign trip.' I explained to him that a trip within the country would probably cost as much in airfares alone. The patriarch replied, 'It is not about the cost. It is what this kind of behaviour does to damage our company's culture. We are a fifty-year old company—not some startup where this kind of behaviour is encouraged.'

IS FLIPPING A COIN A MORE ACCURATE HIRING METHOD?

To answer this question you have to compare the rate of successful hiring and the probability of successful hiring by flipping a coin. We all know that when you toss a coin, there is a 50 per cent chance of doing something right (or wrong). It is worth examining through this case what happened when a company actually decided to carry out this analysis.

CASE

A Fortune 50 company wanted to evaluate the hiring ability of the CEO and his eight direct reportees over a year. The trigger was the unusually high rate of failure of the new hires at the CEO's direct reportees and the people who reported to them. The CEO was convinced that the staffing team was incompetent and was not doing a good job.

This company was a top paymaster and with their awesome brand pull as an employer, they had no difficulty poaching the 'best of the best' talent from the industry. The staffing team's motto was to hire only the 'best of the best'. Every new hire would be hailed as the next big superstar and the announcement would be sent out to the employees. A quarter after being hired, the CEO would tone down his enthusiasm and say that while the new hire was good, he was taking time to adjust to the high-performance culture. Another quarter later, the verdict would be clear: the new hire was not shaping up and was to be watched closely for a quarter. If the person failed to live up to the expectations, the person would be asked to leave. A quarter later, inevitably, most of the 'superstars' would be asked to go for non-performance.

The HR leader said, 'It is hard to hire the right person. I am never given a job description before I hire. So I brief the search firms based on what I think is right. The CEO tells me, 'You are the head of HR. You should know what we are looking for. I just want you to hire a "rock star". We are the best paymasters. You should have no problems hiring the best of the best.' So the HR leader would try and poach someone who had worked with the top consulting firm or the top firm of different sectors. The interview comments for most candidates were limited to cryptic phrases like, 'Hire this guy. He is a rock star.'

The HR leader kept on insisting on detailed written comments made during the interview and compared them with comments recorded in the performance appraisal of the candidate. He also started asking the interviewers the questions they had asked during the interview that helped them get insights about the candidate's capabilities. For example: The interviewer asked, 'Where do you see yourself in five years?' Answer: 'I want to be the CEO of this company.' The interviewer concluded that the candidate was a high achiever and ambitious. A year later the person's performance appraisal recorded that this new hire had unrealistic expectations and his performance was below average. This would be a case of wrong hiring. Another leader had asked a candidate, 'If you could be an animal, which animal would you be?' The candidate who answered that he saw himself as a dog was chosen because the interviewer believed that when someone identifies with canines, they are going to be extremely loyal. The candidate, however, did not last long enough to prove his loyalty since he was asked to leave on grounds of poor performance.

In contrast, a successful hire was defined as one where the assessments were similar. So if the interviewer had written that the candidate was very articulate and displayed strong domain knowledge and this is what was stated in the performance appraisal a year after the person was hired, it would count as a successful hire. When the study was completed the results were shocking. With the exception of one leader who had a success rate of one in three candidates, most leaders had a hiring success rate of 8 per cent to 10 per cent on an average. That meant that 90 per cent of the hiring decisions being made by them were wrong.

Just remember that if they were to toss a coin and choose a candidate on that basis, the law of probability tells us that they would be right 50 per cent of the time. I strongly recommend that you study the hiring effectiveness of your top team using this simple approach. You will know how effective your hiring methods are.

THE COST OF A WRONG HIRE AT THE TOP

To calculate the price of a wrong hire at the top, take this list and fill up the figures for the last wrong hire you made:

1. Notice pay (averages about two months and could be as high as six months' pay for senior level hires),
2. Fee paid to the search firm (varies from 5 per cent to 35 per cent of the salary of the new hire),
3. Relocation expenses,
4. The cost of picking up notice pay paid to the previous employer and
5. Outplacement fees (if paid).

The biggest cost of a wrong hire lies in the hidden costs that are very difficult to quantify. While the staffing department will count the gap between the last day of employment of the wrong hire to the date of joining of the new hire, the correct way to account for the cost is to look at the last date when an incumbent fully handled the role successfully and the first day when an incumbent performs the role fully. Add to this the following costs:

1. Cost of missed deadlines,
2. Cost of lost clients,
3. Cost of additional hiring to be done—this happens when the outgoing employee takes a string of loyalists with him or her,
4. Low morale arising out of the actions of the wrong hire and
5. Loss of intellectual property or competitive knowledge.

Once you total the cost you will discover that it is better to invest in understanding how to hire the right person than to pay the cost which varies anywhere from one-and-a-half times of the person's salary to as much as five to eight times the annual salary in case of a senior-level hire.

And don't forget to add the time that will be spent in hiring the next person, the assessment costs, the time spent in interviews, etc., and the scary thought that you could once again land up making a hiring mistake.

IDEAS

1. Limiting the hiring process to what is stated in the candidate's resume does not work in case of hiring senior-level candidates. The CV is a listing of qualifications and work experience that is more relevant as a predictor of success at junior levels. At senior levels, the person has to navigate through a lot of ambiguity. This is where the personality factors affect the choices the leader will make.
2. In senior-level roles, the educational qualification and previous work experience are not any predictors of success. It is the personality of the individual—both the 'bright side' and 'dark side' that helps us predict success in the role. The personality when assessed can give us insights into the person's fit for the demands of the role.
3. The individual's values and motives provide us the potential fit with the organization's culture. These assessments are difficult to carry out without using standardized psychological instruments that are reliable and have been validated by a large cross section of leaders.

5

Hiring Leaders Needs a Different Approach

In April 2001, the organization and leadership practice of McKinsey came up with the phrase 'war for talent' when they said,

> 'Having great managerial talent has always been important, but now it is critical. In today's competitive knowledge-based world, the caliber of a company's talent increasingly determines success in the marketplace. At the same time, attracting and retaining great talent is becoming more difficult, as demand for highly skilled people outstrips supply. The war for talent will persist for at least the next two decades. The forces that are causing it are deep and powerful. The war for talent is a business reality.'

This idea has proved to be extremely prophetic. Wherever you look, there is a great demand for talented people. People who have the right level of skills and a proven track record and also a 'great attitude' are hard to find. Businesses are getting more competitive and complex.

Business leaders constantly worry that they do not have enough people who can run their increasingly complex organizations in multiple countries, with fickle consumers and volatile commodity markets.

What is interesting is that the small entrepreneur feels as helpless as a large Fortune 500 corporation when it comes to the process of hiring the right person at the leadership level. A small- or medium-scale firm has very few people besides the owner in such key positions and hence a single wrong hire can jeopardize the entire business. Yet organizations continue to hire people based on what I very politely call a social conversation. Most interviewers ask the same set of questions to candidates regardless of the role for which they are being interviewed.

A MORE EXPERIENCED CANDIDATE IS NOT NECESSARILY BETTER

Let us take a situation where a hiring decision could be the difference between life and death. Imagine a loved one who is going in for surgery. You have to decide between a surgeon who is highly experienced, say, with twenty years of experience and a surgeon with two years of experience. That would be easy: you will choose a person with twenty years of experience because the person would have built her skill through repeated practice. What would you do if you were to choose between a surgeon with fifteen years of experience and one who has thirty years of experience? If you apply the same criteria, you risk making a wrong choice.

A recent research quoted in the January 2012 issue of the *British Medical Journal* shows that the most experienced surgeons were not the best. It says: 'We observed a concave association between surgeons' experience and their case mix adjusted performance, suggesting that surgeons aged thirty-five to fifty years provided the safest care.'

A surgeon cannot achieve or maintain top performance passively by accumulating years of experience. This raises concerns about ongoing training and motivation throughout a career that extends over decades. Solutions to help surgeons avoid poor outcomes could include simulation and proctoring in the early years of their careers, continuous monitoring of performance and targeted retraining if appropriate. Individual feedback based on outcome indicators might increase awareness about performance and improve safety in surgical practice.

The ability to keep learning throughout one's career is directly correlated to the motivation level of a person. We continue to learn and improve ourselves in tasks that we enjoy and are motivated to do throughout our lives.

WHAT IMPACTS THE HIRING PROCESS?

There are many factors that may determine how successful the new hire will be. When you think of hiring someone for a role, I recommend a short meeting between the stakeholders to discuss the following parameters that are discussed here.

Business Environment

The business environment is dynamic. There was a time when the long-term strategic plans for a business were made to set directions for five years. Today, most businesses create long-term strategic plans for two years since changes in the political, economic and social scenario can change the relevance of the best-crafted plans. So a leader who was very successful in a certain business environment may suddenly become labelled a 'poor or average performer'. Some organizations actually use their talent planning sessions to see if they would rehire the incumbent into the role or if the person's strength is better leveraged in another. When I suggest this to business leaders, they often point out that such a practice would create instability in the organization. My answer is that this exercise gives a chance to find the best opportunity to leverage the strengths of the executive in a new role without waiting for him to fail and then move out as a failure. The requirements of the roles change as the business environment changes. The role of the project manager that you are hiring this year may need different competencies and personality elements to be successful in another year when the business environment changes.

CASE

Harsh G. was the sales head of a cosmetics company. He was viewed as a high achiever and a role model for the way he had established the sales and distribution system across the country. That was until the last quarter of 2008. The market was slowing down everywhere, and for the first time Harsh was struggling to get his numbers. Nothing that he did seemed to go right. The company replaced him with a new hire. Harsh was given a special project to be done at the Mumbai headquarters. When the new hire struggled to meet his numbers, there was some discussion in the leadership team whether they had been quick to write off Harsh, but it was too

> late. Ever since he was sidelined, Harsh had become a shadow of his former self and eventually quit the company. After a few quarters of declining sales, the new hire too quit. I am told the next sales head did better. But then so did the economy!

The landscape in which an organization operates, changes over time. The economic scenario, an evolving base of consumers, technology and disruptive innovation all create forces that need to be continuously managed for someone to be successful. There are factors that affect an individual that may shift the tenuous connection between the individual and a perfectly matched role.

At any given point of time, the match between the individual and the organization is subject to forces of change. So it is easy to understand why a person who has been very successful may progressively start to struggle when the market forces change. On the other hand someone who was written off for being just another average performer may turn out to be the ideal candidate for the role in the new scenario.

Changing Pool of Talent

Search firms will tell you that it is extremely difficult to find the right candidates at the top even for firms that operate in relatively stable environments. The problem is compounded when they are hiring for firms that are entering sunrise industries or technologies that have had no precedence. They are then forced to take people whose skills and experience are transferrable. This creates an obvious risk of failure that the experience and approaches that worked very well in a consumer goods company may not be as effective in a company that is venturing into green energy. Very often it is not the transferability of the new leader's business knowledge that drives failure; it could be the ability to adjust to the culture of the parent company or the expectations of the venture capitalists. If the leader has to attract talent at the campus, the ability to connect to the potential employees will play a major role in the success of the organization. The hiring process needs to factor in this element while assessing the personality of the candidates.

Shifting Labour Markets and Regulations

The rising wages for leadership roles in India combined with the slowing economy in Europe and parts of the US have made it possible for many firms to hire non-resident Indians (NRIs) and foreign nationals for roles based out of India. While most of them are assessed for their work experience and global exposure, the firms rarely ever assess them on the personality fit with the Indian corporate environment. The skill of building relations is important when adjusting to new cultures. A study of 8,474 expatriates from Penn State's Smeal College of Business published in the *Academy of Management Journal* in 2005 had concluded that cultural adjustment is 'perhaps the strongest determinant of disengagement and withdrawal decisions'.

David Harrison and his co-authors clearly state, 'A general, positive, job attitude leads individuals to contribute rather than withhold desirable inputs from their work roles. In view of the current work, we forward that, along with general cognitive ability, a sound measurement of overall job attitude is one of the most useful pieces of information an organization can have about its employees.' (Harrison, 2006)

> Where leadership skills, technical competence and domestic track record were viewed as the prime selection criteria until the 1990s, senior executives in 2005 considered the ability to control emotions as more important than technical skills.

Hiring is Not about Asking Questions

Many interviewers believe that an interview is all about asking questions that stump the candidate. There are books written about questions and puzzles asked during an interview. The question has to help the interviewer get information about the relevant knowledge the person can use to answer a question.

'How do you plan to market it so as to achieve 100 million customers for our email service in six months?' If this question is asked to a candidate for a product manager's role in a company that is launching an email service, it can be a good trigger to give you a glimpse of the creativity of the person. It may also give you insights about how the person deals with the unknown. Yet this may not be the best way to assess someone for the head of manufacturing in a medium-sized company or the CFO of your organization.

The interviewer's skill lies in knowing what to look for in the answer. It is not about asking a question just because you came across a site that had questions like 'Please spell "diverticulitis".' Or 'Room, desk and car—which do you, clean first?' (Glassdoor, 2011). Always ask yourself, what we are trying to assess and how the answer to the question I am asking will help me assess that competency.

Find the Right Methodology to Assess

Adam Bryant has written about the hiring secrets and quirks of CEOs in his book *The Corner Office.* (Bryant, 2011) His research shows the five things most CEOs look for when they hire: (i) passionate curiosity, (ii) battle-hardened confidence, (iii) team smarts, (iv) simple mindset and (v) fearlessness. Yet when you read the fine print, many of them rely on conversations or their own thumb rules to identify these characteristics. Somebody measures confidence by the strength of the handshake. Some measure how long the audience maintains eye contact with the speaker to assess the candidate's skills in working in a team.

A CEO of a large company told me once that he gets put off if he meets a candidate who is not wearing polished shoes. Imagine yourself as a candidate being assessed on the basis of your handshake (or some such criteria) in one company. The other company uses a scientifically proven assessment tool in hiring. Which one do you think will give you the result you will be comfortable with even if it is in your favour? This book tries to suggest a standardized option to assess people and what that would measure.

IDEAS

1. The war for talent has made it hard to find people at any level, especially at the top, where the price of a wrong hire is enormous. Hiring has to become a very important tool to ensure that the organization has the right talent. More and more people have to learn to hire right. The interview needs to be structured to ensure it yields the data needed to assess the candidate's fit with the organization's culture. To really get it right, use a proven assessment technique.
2. The business context is a big factor that determines the success or failure of leaders. Just like you build strategic plans for the business that lay out a plan based on a two-year time frame, you may like to consider 'rehiring' a leader every two years. This will ensure that the leader's skills and personality factors are still relevant to be effective in the changing scenario.
3. Do not pick up questions off a book on interviewing or from the Internet just because you found them fascinating. Do not get carried away by these clever questions because some well-known company uses them to hire. Every hiring situation is different. Each interview question is an opportunity to assess a specific aspect of the person's fit to the role or the organizational culture. So do not waste it on frivolous questions. You have to know what you are trying to assess by the question and if that is the best way to assess.

6

Interviewers' Mistakes

Dan Gilbert, author of *Stumbling on Happiness*, says,

> 'When our bathroom scale delivers bad news, we hop off and then on again, just to make sure we didn't misread the display or put too much pressure on one foot. When our scale delivers good news, we smile and head for the shower. By uncritically accepting evidence when it pleases us and insisting on more when it doesn't, we subtly tip the scales in our favour.' (Gilbert, 2006)

That isn't just the way we weigh ourselves in the bathroom. We weigh evidence the same way. Decision makers don't realize just how easily and often their objectivity is compromised. The human brain knows many tricks that allow it to consider evidence, weigh facts and still reach precisely the conclusion it favours. Think of what that means in case of hiring. Unless people become conscious about the myths that drive them to make mistakes, they can never fix the problems. As they say, awareness is the first step towards improving.

Hiring at the top requires a lot more of planning and

skill to get it right. The stakes are higher and the mistakes could plunge a company into the deep end. Popular press is full of examples of well-known business leaders who have their own recipes on how to hire the right person. In an interview to *The New York Times,* Howard Schultz, CEO of Starbucks shares his recipe, 'First off, I want to know what you're reading and then I'll ask you why. Tell me what work-life balance means to you.' (Perina, Flora & Marano, 2012)

When interviewers do not use structured and scientific approaches in identifying candidates, they could make decisions based on conversations that are no more than social chats. They need to see not only candidates who have previous experience that they could leverage but also find those who have the potential to perform effectively in jobs that are not aligned with past experiences.

Social media startup company ONEsite says, 'Some of our best developers have been classics majors and physicists with no previous programming experience. They were able to apply their knowledge of other 'languages' to think structurally and logically.' The popular airlines JetBlue looks for people who have a background in law enforcement because safety and service matters when it comes to hiring the in-flight crew. Megan White, director of talent acquisition says, 'Approximately 10% of our in-flight crew is made up of former law enforcement officials. We have many ex-firefighters too. Their expertise aligns well with the culture at JetBlue.' Google does not always look for software geeks when they hire. They look for people who have overcome odds and demonstrate tenacity. One recent hire traded a nonprofit job in Africa—where he faced down a cohort of Namibian generals while performing HIV research—for a spot in Google's human-resources analytics department. 'Someone who can take on big problems and not be scared—those are the people who are compelling,' says Google Hiring Manager Todd Carlisle. Not that you have to save the world: Carlisle says he was recently impressed by a woman who worked nights as a seamstress to support her sister through college. (Lee, 2010)

Structured approaches in interviewing can help us identify people who may not have had the qualification or experience in doing a particular job. The interview, if conducted by a trained person can help us identify the candidate's potential to do the task. It is also possible to assess if the person has the psychological makeup needed to succeed. This means, for example, those candidates who have no sales experience can exhibit the dimensions necessary for success in a sales job by answering questions around their ability to persuade others in contexts related to non-sales.

While an organization may not be willing to put together an elaborate hiring process for blue-collar employees or employees even at the middle level, at the senior level, getting the right person hired can make a big difference. Entrepreneurs cite lack of talent as their single biggest barrier to developing their business. They have just a handful of leaders in their senior leadership team. So it is as important to get hiring right at the senior level in a small organization as it is for a large corporation. The margin of error has to be minimized.

COMMON MISTAKES BY INTERVIEWERS

Unclear Expectations of the Interviewers

When putting the job description together for a vacancy, you will come up with a 'wish list' of skills, qualifications, experience, interests and personality traits for an ideal candidate. Multiple interviewers often describe the same job very differently. As a result there is no consistency in their articulation of knowing what competencies will be needed to be successful. This will result in a very broad set of competencies that can only be fulfilled by someone possessing the skills of a superhero. The best way to resolve this problem is to get all of them into one room and jointly analyse the demands of the role. The competencies should naturally emerge from that.

Articulation Bias

It is easy to get dazzled by someone's ability to articulate his ideas well. Socially skilled people can very often come across as charming and leading the employer to assuming that if a person is articulate, he will 'learn what he does not know'; because it is assumed that the articulate person is very smart. This halo effect will let an interviewer assume that the person has all the other competencies needed for the role. The converse is also true. There are enough studies that show that a competent person who is not articulate may be looked at as unsuitable while an incompetent but articulate person is often viewed as suitable for a role. The CEO of a major TV network Abbe Raven says, 'Number one, for me, is instinct. It's all about who they are as a person, their chemistry, their charisma and their gravitas.'

The chairman of a major software company told me that he could always 'spot a rock star based on the confidence demonstrated'. Charisma and compassion are often easy to fake in a freewheeling approach to hiring. It may have little to do with the competencies needed for the job. You don't want to hire someone who can answer your question but cannot perform the role.

Playing Psychologist

'If you were to be an animal which animal would you be?' Asking the question in a social gathering could lead to some interesting conversation. What is worse is when the candidate says that he would love to be a bulldog; the interviewer makes a mental note that classifies the candidate as having traits of loyalty and persistence. These beliefs are no more scientific than deciding that people with a certain colour of eyes are more intelligent than others. Since the objective of playing psychologist is to have a view of the candidate's personality, why not use personality assessments to do exactly the same. (In a later chapter we shall discuss personality elements in greater detail.)

Not Taking Notes

It is hard for people to remember what was asked as a question and what the candidate answered. As a result some important follow-up questions may be missed. When there is a long time gap between the date of the interview and the decision, interviewers often forget important details that will help them compare their insights about different candidates. Not taking notes makes it hard for interviewers to improve their skills. They will never know whether they asked the right questions or whether they drew the right conclusion based on the answers given by the candidate.

Overlap in Competencies Covered

It is a good idea to have at least one more interviewer check for a competency. What does not work is when several interviewers cover the same competency. In that case if there are other critical competencies to be probed, the panel may have to decide with little or no information.

Example: 'Tell me about a time when you had to make an unpopular decision.' 'Have you had to make a decision that many employees did not like and were opposed to?' 'Tell me about a time when you had to convince employees about a decision that you made which was resisted by the employees.' All of them will yield data about the same competency.

Not Checking for Role Fit

The biggest limitation of an interviewer is to assume that just because someone has the qualifications and experience to do the role, he is motivated to do it. Do not assume that every engineer who has graduated with honours from a top-notch engineering college wants to build a career as an engineer. Just look at the number of engineer-MBAs in any business school and you will know what I mean. Taking this argument further, although the person has the credentials and experience to be an engineer, he might not be motivated to be one after a few years as an engineer. So many technologists wish to switch to managerial roles. I have come across so many managers who yearn to go back to an individual contributor role. A celebrated scientist with three patents to her credit told me that all she ever wanted to do was to be a violinist. At the senior level, it is equally important to assess whether the candidate is motivated to continue to work in a role she is qualified to perform and have the experience to do the same.

Not Checking for Culture Fit

The senior executives' success greatly depends on their ability to fit in with the underlying cultural assumptions of the organization. What may be viewed as strong bonhomie within the team, can be viewed as flamboyant and inappropriate in another organization. The candidate's values and the organizational values must match in order for the person to succeed. Interviewers often get dazzled by the qualifications of candidates especially when they are acquired from top-notch institutions. When candidates show that they have worked for high-profile organizations, the interviewers tend to get swayed by the credentials and assume that such a highly qualified person having such an enviable track record will automatically be successful. At senior levels the 'fit' is the reason why a new hire succeeds, not the qualifications and experience. The personality characteristics that make someone successful in one organization may be the very cause of failure to be accepted in another. Offering an opinion on a subject regardless of expertise or previous experience could be viewed as being foolhardy in one organization and show the person in positive light as a risk-taker in another.

The interviewing panel members can make a big difference to the final outcome of the hiring process. It involves being clear about what the requirements of the role are, understanding the fit of the person with the culture of the organization and finding the most appropriate ways of measuring this.

IDEAS

1. Interviewing is a skill that can be learnt and improved upon through rigorous practice. Not everyone is going to be a good Interviewer. Do you know who the interviewers in your organization are who can successfully identify the candidate who will be successful in your culture?
2. Interviewers have to spend time identifying the requirements of the role. That has four components: the qualifications required to perform the role, the experience needed, the competencies that are critical to the role and the personality elements that will be needed to be successful. This is called a Success Profile℠ and will be described in detail in the next chapter.
3. The 'fit' of the personality with the requirements of the role and the organization's culture contributes hugely to a candidate's success. This needs to be done using the right tool and by a trained assessor. In a subsequent chapter I shall describe one of the tools that I have used to assess personality and how that can be a useful guide for you.

SECTION 2

7

Building a Success Profile℠

Let us imagine that you want someone to buy a shirt on your behalf. You mention your favourite brand of shirts and ask your friend to buy it for you. You may find a problem with the fit because the shirt is too tight or too loose for you. You may find many more things wrong with it. The colour may not be what you want. It may turn out to be something you could wear to a party and not to office. The buttons may be too flashy. There may be too many or too few pockets. The design of the pocket could be strange. You get the drift. The more precisely you think of what matters to you the more likely you will choose a shirt that is right for you. In case of hiring for a top-level job, you definitely need to specify what matters by creating a Success Profile℠. This answers the question: what will make the person successful in that role and be a good fit in the culture of the organization.

If you do not know where you are going, you can never get lost. While hiring someone at the leadership level, if you do not have a yardstick against which you will measure the candidates, you will be forced to select the best candidate, which usually means someone with an impressive resume.

At the leadership level, you need to hire the 'right' person, not the best. To find the right person, we need to find the fit with the role and the organizational culture.

A job description lists the major job responsibilities, knowledge and experience the role needs. I have often asked fellow practitioners if they use job descriptions before hiring. Most job descriptions are often out of date. Check out a few in your organization if you do not believe me. The task of updating job descriptions is given to someone in the HR department—the most popular choice being assigning it to the summer trainee from a business school. So they are neither current nor useful in hiring.

Some business leaders say that they use competencies to the job description. Competencies refer to the *behaviour* that has to be demonstrated in order to be successful in a job or role. This document is then used as a yardstick while hiring a candidate.

A Success Profile^{SM} has the four elements: education, work experience, competencies and personality factors needed to succeed in a role. This is a comprehensive document that should be used to identify what to look for while assessing the candidate for the role. Missing out a few elements here may be the difference between failure and success. The next case is all about the importance of highlighting the key factors of a role:

CASE

A very large process manufacturing company in India acquired a manufacturing plant in Mexico. The Mexican plant had a history of financial trouble and labour unrest and had lost the trust of the employees as well as the financial institutions. What kept it going was strong technical skills. The Mexican company had a reputation of having the best engineering and technical talent in the country.

The Success Profile℠ said that the ideal candidate would have deep engineering skills and significant strength in influencing skills.

The final choice was between one candidate from India who was an engineer from IIT and had a doctoral degree in materials engineering and another candidate who was from Mexico and had a master's degree in physics. The second candidate was extremely strong in influencing skills. His communication style was authentic, and that made it easy for people to trust him. If you had to choose one of these candidates as country head, based on just these two pieces of information, whom would you vote for?

The main question for the hiring committee was to debate whether having an engineering degree would increase the probability of success more than a candidate who was strong in influencing others but lacked the technical depth. You would probably say that given the challenge of labour unrest, etc., the board would vote in favour of influencing skills. Technical skills could very easily be supplemented by having a good team of engineers support this person. But that was not the decision the board took.

The board voted for the person with a Ph.D in materials engineering. They felt that the technical skills of this person would give them an edge in the market. The candidate took up the challenge and relocated to Mexico. But he was unable to gain the confidence of the union and the bankers. The new technology that he wanted to introduce was a failure because of the labour unrest that continued to plague him.

WHY BUILD A SUCCESS PROFILE℠

A job description gets us a listing of the qualifications and experience. That is probably enough if you are looking to hire people at the junior level when the stakes are low and the replacement cost of a wrong hire is limited. At the middle management level, it is important to evaluate the competencies the role requires. That means we should start to focus more deeply on assessing competencies besides evaluating the education and work experience. While hiring someone at the leadership level the two left boxes in the diagram, that is, education and experience are table stakes. I would even venture to put a number to it and say that it contributes barely 20 per cent to a leader's success. At the senior level, the competencies and personality matter disproportionately more. A Success Profile℠ captures all the four elements that a senior leader needs.

Success Profile℠ is the term used by DDI, a firm that specializes in selection and assessments. I have just adapted their terms. These four areas are the ones you must assess in a hiring decision.

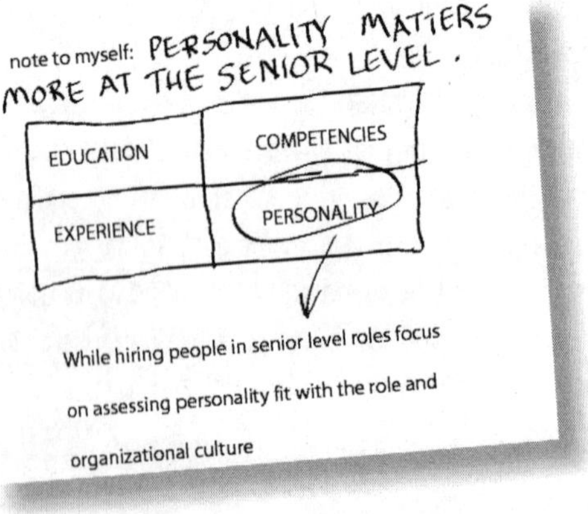

Education: Here you have to list the technical or professional information the person must know to complete the task. Education will tell you what the person knows.

Experience: This tells us the educational and work achievements needed to successfully perform job activities. It tells us the circumstances under which the person has applied his qualifications in the real world.

Competencies: This refers to the behaviours that have to be exhibited while doing the job successfully. When a person moves from being a functional leader (e.g., head of marketing or finance) to being a business leader (i.e., head of a strategic business unit or a CEO), some of the competencies required may be different for the roles.

Personality: This is usually the most neglected and yet the most important part of senior-level hiring success. Different elements of personality will affect motivational fit with the role, and the values help us find a fit with the organizational culture.

Let us try to build a Success Profile℠ of the CEO of a mid-size company. I have used this role to illustrate the value of this process in improving hiring success at the senior level. At this level it is worth taking the trouble to build one for each role. These need to be updated at least once every year because the business environment changes sufficiently in a year to demand changes in the Success Profile℠. Look at the listing of top companies around the world for this year. See how many of the top ten companies exist in the same list that is a year or two older. If the business environment and competitive scenario changes rapidly, the Success Profile^{SM} needs to reflect the new demands. What you expected in a role a year back may not matter today. A person who deliberates and analyses all the possibility for a long time before committing resources may have been a successful leader two years back. Someone who is more adaptable and a greater risk taker may be what the company needs today. The personality factors that would enable a person to succeed may be roadblocks in a reconfigured competitive scenario.

HOW TO BUILD A SUCCESS PROFILE^{SM}

Let us use the DDI approach to build an actual Success Profile^{SM}. We will build it for a CEO of a mid-size company. You will notice that I have not mentioned the qualifications and experience needed. In my opinion at the senior level, the interviewers must be capable of assessing the competencies based on the business drivers. There must be an articulation of the personality elements that would be enablers and those that would be derailers in the role. All personality factors have to be seen in the context of a role and the organizational culture. The role in turn is defined by the business drivers.

What follows is the example of how the Success Profile^{SM} of a CEO was built by a firm. This approach can help you create one for any role that you are hiring for.

The Business Context

The previous CEO had retired and the promoters had given the mandate to find them a new CEO.

The company had been struggling in the marketplace. For years there was a steady base of customers that kept eroding because of the company's dropping standards of service. While the market for the product had expanded, the brand has not remained on top of the customer's mind according to a recent brand perception survey. The company's market share had slipped from being the second largest to sixth position in a span of four years. The leadership team was demotivated. Every meeting of the leadership team would result in a blame game. The sales head would blame the low sales to poor brand recognition and unattractive pricing. The CFO would blame the sales team for not being aggressive enough. The marketing head would ascribe low brand awareness to inconsistent messaging driven by low funds. She would often share figures of the competitor's advertising and communication budget. The HR director would share the results of low employee morale as the reason why the company was not doing well. Meanwhile, new players had entered the market and introduced additional features in the product backed by a strong after-sales service philosophy.

If this is the business context, here are the next steps if you wish to create a Success Profile^{SM} for the role:

Steps

Step 1: Identify the Key Drivers of the Business

Four key drivers had been identified, which the new CEO would have to address:

1. Build and enhance the brand,
2. Create a customer-centric organization,

3. Create alignment in the leadership team and
4. Drive profit.

Step 2: Identify the Competencies Needed for Each Driver

For each driver, two to three competencies have to be identified. The list of competencies was identified as follows:

1. Build and enhance the brand:
   » Craft vision for the business and get employee buy-in,
   » Customer centricity,
   » Develop people to succeed in the new scenario.
2. Create a customer-centric organization:
   » Empower teams to take decisions on the ground,
   » Delegate,
   » Deliver results.
3. Create alignment in the organization:
   » Create a road map that energizes the employees,
   » Hold people accountable for results,
   » Build and reward collaboration among teams.
4. Drive profits
   » Financial acumen,
   » Business acumen,
   » Entrepreneurial decision making.

Step 3: Identify the Personality Elements that will Enable or Derail the New Hire

The following behaviours will be enabling success:

1. Ability to see the big picture,

2. Creative,
3. High energy,
4. Quick decision making,
5. Strong people skills.

The following behaviours will be barriers to success:

1. Rigid and hierarchical,
2. Excessively independent (someone who does not involve others),
3. Indecisive.

Step 4: Consolidate the Competencies and Personality Factors to Show the Road Map to Success

This final step will also serve as a road map for the new hire. It tells the person what is expected. This makes the document an extremely useful guide for evaluating progress of the new hire. It also serves as a yardstick to measure developmental opportunities and where exactly a person may need coaching help. [Tip: You may like to look at what the previous incumbent did well and what he didn't in order to do a final sanity check on the Success Profile℠.] Here's what it will look like.

Builds Effective Teams

Using appropriate methods and interpersonal styles to develop, motivate and guide the team to attain successful outcomes and business objectives.

Key behaviours to build effective teams:

» Create shared purpose,
» Promote team processes,

» Celebrate success,
» Connect closely with team members.

Business Savvy

He should demonstrate a keen understanding of basic business operations and organizational systems that drive profitable growth.

Key behaviours that demonstrate business savvy:

» Focus on key business levers,
» Create information systems,
» Focus on decision-making processes,
» Evaluate high-risk and high-opportunity decisions.

Establishing Strategic Direction

Establishing and committing to a long-term business direction based on an analysis of systemic information and consideration of resources, market drivers and organizational values.

Key behaviours that demonstrate a compelling road map:

» Build information systems,
» Understand system interdependencies,
» Select the high-impact strategic priorities,
» Identify short- and long-term goals.

Communicating Vision

Vividly communicating a compelling view of the future state in a way that helps others understand and feel how business outcomes will be different when the vision and values become a reality.

Key behaviours to communicate vision:

» Personalize the vision and its benefits for each employee,
» Inspire others to contribute to the vision.

Customer Focus

Ensuring that the customer perspective is a driving force behind business decisions and activities; crafting and implementing service practices that meet customers' and own organization's needs.

Key behaviours that demonstrate customer centricity:

» Seek information to understand customer,
» Identify systems to impact customer service and retention,
» Create processes to ensure customer satisfaction.

Delivering Results

Driving high standards for individual, team and organizational accomplishment; tenaciously working to meet or exceed challenging goals; deriving satisfaction from goal achievement and continuous improvement.

Key behaviours that will help deliver results:

» Set challenging goals for self and others,
» Persist to completion by daily focus on results.

Developing People

Establishing systems and processes to attract, develop, engage and retain talented individuals; creating a work environment where people can realize their full potential, thus allowing the organization to meet current and future business challenges.

Key behaviours that develop people:

» Determine talent mix needed to achieve strategy,
» Assess the talent pipeline,
» Craft developmental assignments that build individual confidence and organizational capability,
» Pay for performance philosophy,
» Retain talented individuals.

Delegation

Share authority and responsibilities with others to move decision making and accountability lower down the organization.

Key behaviours to improve delegation:

» Promote risk taking,
» Provide resources to support the individual,
» Monitor progress and issues.

Entrepreneurship

Using understanding of key market drivers to create and seize business opportunities, expand into new markets and launch innovative products and services.

Key behaviours that enhance entrepreneurship:

» Build external focus of leaders,
» Evaluate high-potential business opportunities,
» Encourage experimentation and risks.

Financial Acumen

Utilizing financial data to diagnose business, keeping a financial perspective in the forefront as strategic decisions are made.

Key behaviours to demonstrate financial acumen:

» Analyse key indicators of financial health,
» Identify implications of financial trends for the organization,
» Use financial data to guide strategic and operational decision making.

Accountability

Translate strategic priorities into operational reality—aligning communication, accountabilities, resource capabilities, internal processes and ongoing measurement systems to ensure that strategic priorities yield measurable and sustainable results.

Key behaviours to build accountability:

» Translate initiatives into actions,
» Implement communication strategy,
» Create role clarity and authority to act,
» Ensure skills and readiness,
» Align systems and process,
» Create measurement discipline.

Decision Making

Securing and comparing information from multiple sources to identify business issues; committing to an action after weighing alternative solutions against important decision criteria.

Key behaviours to build accountability:

» Understand possible cause–effect relationships,
» Select the best of alternatives,
» Make timely decisions,
» Involve others in the decision-making process.

While creating a Success Profile℠, you should also keep in mind the various stakeholders (internal and external) that the new hire will have to deal with. In case of a CEO it could be the board or the chairman. It would include the ministries, external union leaders, media, etc. The internal stakeholders would include other members of

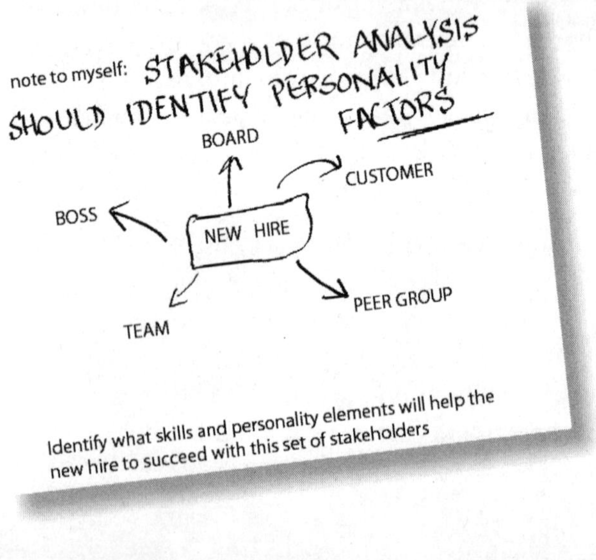

the management team, the members of the global team or corporate office, etc. Speak to the person who is doing the job (even if it is someone temporarily holding fort till the new person is hired), speak to the person who manages those who will do this role, speak to others who can detail what business strategies are now needed to be successful as a business and more specifically in that role.

A SUCCESS PROFILE℠ FOR EVERY ROLE?

Is it worth creating a Success Profile℠ for every role? At the senior leadership level, it is absolutely worth it. If you cannot do it, ask the other leaders to create one. Ask your HR leader to work with you to create one.

It helps to create a common understanding of what would create success in the role. That can be the basis of promoting someone to that role. It can be used for developing leaders. It helps in hiring someone and also during the performance appraisal discussions. At the level of the CEO and his direct reportees it is absolutely necessary to fix the standards.

I must end with a caveat. It is easy to find a long list of competencies to look for in each role. Once you have drawn up the document, prioritize the two or three major competencies, enablers and derailers. That is a realistic starting point. If it is a choice between perfection and simplicity, I am in favour of simplicity. Build a quick prototype and see if it flies!

IDEAS

1. A Success Profile^{SM} must reflect what it takes to be successful in your current and future business scenario. Start by creating the Success Profile^{SM} of the senior roles in the organization. It begins by having a discussion on what makes someone succeed and fail in the role. Identify the education, experience, competencies and personal attributes required for job success.
2. Understand the business environment, goals and objectives associated with the role. Now ask what knowledge, skills, motivations and competencies will enable people to be successful. Keep the discussion limited to the behaviours that the person must demonstrate, when you say, for example, 'The person must be a good team player.' List down what behaviour would you see in a good team player doing the role.
3. Revisit these profiles every year. Business environments change. The factors that will make someone successful will change to reflect the business environment. The Success Profile^{SM} should be used to decide the developmental inputs and coaching the new hire may be needed to bridge the gaps. The developmental inputs can help bridge competency gaps.

8

Personality and 'Fit'

Once you have the Success Profile[SM] worked out you know the kind of education, experience, competencies and personality the new hire must have to be successful. Before hiring someone, would you like to know if that person is easy to manage, hard-working, cooperative, and good with customers, thorough, innovative and quick to learn your business? Before investing in their development, would you like to know more about the person's strengths, weaknesses, preferred learning methods and even the core values and motivations? These questions can be answered only if you measure personality. That requires someone to use the right psychometric tool and someone trained on interpreting the results.

CASE

Janet is the marketing head of a well-known consumer goods company. She is revered as one of the most creative minds in Asia. She has the Midas touch they say. She has worked across categories from food to apparel to cosmetics. She can be seen, featured on the

> cover of some magazine or the other every now and then. Her boss just does not know how to handle her. She can fly off the handle during a meeting, burst into tears and resign from the company—all on the same day. A few hours later she will be seen sitting in the office working till the wee hours to send off a campaign that is being launched on television channels. Her boss simply shrugs his shoulder and says he does not know how to deal with her.
>
> The meetings with her team end up at well past midnight. In the meetings she swings from one extreme to another. It is very common to see her walk in to a meeting with a box of chocolates for everyone, roses for the birthday boy or girl. When she is upset with the quality of someone's work, she will scream and humiliate the person till the person breaks down and cries. That is usually a signal for the HR team to start guessing who would be the next person to quit the team. Yet, the team admits that working with Janet for a year value-adds to their professional knowledge more than anything else. The business schools vie with each other to see if she could be persuaded to come and address the students.
>
> During the six years that she has been working at this firm, she has left the company three times to start some project on her own or to just go cycling in the Himalayas. A month or two later she comes back to continue just where she left off. Her boss told me that managing Janet was the same as smoking a packet of cigarettes every hour.

Have you known someone like that? At senior levels, personality is the *most* significant reason why someone fails or succeeds. Yet, even at senior levels so many hiring decisions are made without any form of personality assessment being done. Questions are asked in an interview and we naively believe that the answers will give us insights to assess personality.

Asking someone, 'Tell me about your strengths and weaknesses is not going to leave you any wiser because someone who is a glib talker will exaggerate his strengths and downplay his weaknesses to make them look like strengths. A typical answer about weaknesses that I have heard play out repeatedly is, 'I am a workaholic.' The potential employer secretly chuckles at the joy of having discovered that the new hire will turn out to be ambitious and hard working. The interviewer feels that they will get more than what they are paying for and heave a sigh of relief that the candidate has no developmental gaps that they need to worry about. During the discussion on 'derailers', in a later chapter, we shall see what makes the same candidate appear almost like a different person from the one you hired. You may not change your decision to hire a person just because he is a little shy, but if you knew that this would be a fatal flaw that would come in the way of the person's ability to succeed, maybe you would have chosen differently. Once you know the demands of the role based on the Success Profile℠ you have drawn up, it is important to assess the personality of the candidate to know: Does the person have unpredictable mood swings and loses his temper under stress? Does the person keep asking for more data and more proof and almost seems paralysed and afraid to take a decision?

How can we predict that the sales director we intend to hire from our competitor is actually someone who hates meeting people? At senior leadership levels, it is personality factors like this that can be the reason why leaders fail.

Think about the fit between the person and the role as the clothes that the person will be wearing. The clothes need to be of the right size and help the person perform the role comfortably. It would be hard for the person to run while wearing leather shoes and a business suit. In the same way, think of the organization's culture as the occasion, for which the person is dressing up. If the occasion is casual, the dress code will expect the person to wear clothes to suit the evening. A business meeting may require a different attire to be worn, even though the person going for the meeting is the same. Success in hiring is about understanding the link between these three elements: the personality factors of the candidate, the extent of fit with the role and culture of the organization.

The extent of fit determines success. The same person can be successful or fail in another organization depending on a better or worse fit with his personality. Remember the advice about why you should not hire a 'star'? You may have seen someone who was extremely successful in one role fail when they got promoted to a higher

responsibility. We have all been told that every top-notch sales person does not make a great sales manager. That is because the demands of the role are different. The person may fail because he does not have those competencies or the motivational fit with the role or the culture of the organization. If the person is not motivated to do what the job needs him to do, the person cannot be successful no matter how eminently qualified he may be.

The case of Venu that is mentioned below is a great example of a person who was highly qualified and had the necessary work experience that had developed the competencies needed for the role. Of the four elements in the Success Profile℠, Venu was a great fit as far as three of them were concerned. He had the right education, the right work experience and had developed most of the competencies for the role. Notice I said that he had developed 'most' of the competencies. The gaps were because of the elements of personality that were not assessed. Personality elements have a strong influence on the competencies. Venu's case is a good example of this.

CASE

Venu, a chartered accountant, CFA and MBA from one of the top business schools had just been hired from a financial services firm where he was the star at the leadership level. His insights about the market and his timely investment decisions had made the rapidly growing 400-people firm, the envy of the peers and the darling of the media.

When Venu was headhunted to man the top position in the retail banking operation of a well-known conglomerate, the media applauded the group's ability to attract top talent and said that they

> had indeed chosen the right person who could lead their retail bank expansion. When Venu quit that role in less than eighteen months, there was some speculation in the media about a rift at the top of the house. Some speculated that it was hard for an external hire to succeed in the well-entrenched culture of the company. Venu's version was different.
>
> He said, 'The culture of the organization drove me crazy. Every time I travel to a branch, I would spend the day reviewing the operations. In the evening, they would organize cocktails and dinner with the staff. I would rather curl up in bed and read a book while listening to music. The unspoken expectation is that you have to socialize after office hours. That is my free time. I have had to suffer through the same routine of meeting the same people I have spent the whole day with and once again suffer their banal humour and useless chatter. I wish they would show the same enthusiasm on the job. At the head office, every Sunday, I am expected to join the same group of five directors for a game of golf. I have started learning golf and it has helped me improve my concentration. It is the beer drinking session after golf that I dread. I am forced to socialize with this coterie every Sunday. I am not willing to take this torture anymore.'

I am sure, Venu would have come across as pleasant and articulate during the five rounds of interviews the board had with him. They were all amazed by his insights on the industry and were struck by his brilliance. No one expected him to have this aversion for socializing with the employees. No one ever checks for that. During the interview he had come across as articulate and perhaps a little reserved. They had ascribed it to Venu being new to the organization. The directors had made a special effort to include him in their weekend golfing ritual to make

Venu feel at home. After the game they would catch a beer and small talk before they headed home. They were all caught off guard when Venu announced his desire to quit to the press before they even knew what was brewing. The board was left red-faced.

It is quite likely that the interview did not include questions like, 'Do you enjoy socializing with colleagues?' Venu was not motivated to do what the job needed him to do. Interview questions cannot assess personality. It needs someone trained in the appropriate psychometric instrument.

In measuring anything, it is easy to measure what you can see and measure with ease. In case of the Success Profile^SM, it is easy to screen someone on the basis of what appears on the left side, that is, education and experience. Both appear on the CV and are easy

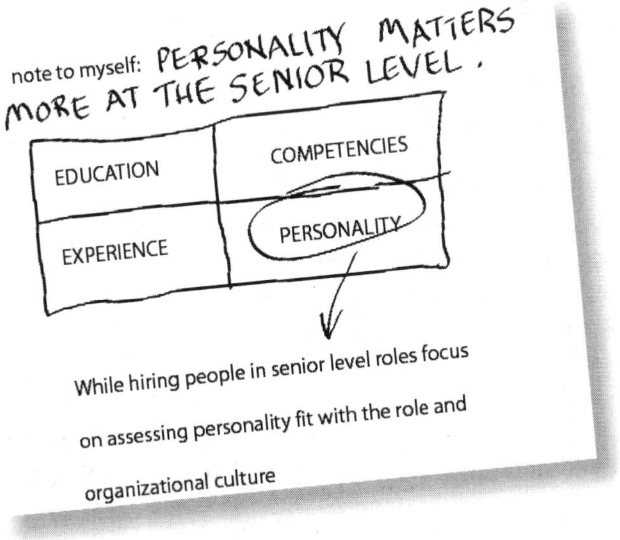

to verify. Competencies will be visible through the behaviour. When the candidate goes about the task, the behaviours that can be seen are the competencies. The candidate's competencies can be evaluated from being a developmental gap to a significant strength.

I have worked in very different kinds of organizations and have had a chance to see the personality types that thrive in different environments.

When I joined an advertising firm I found there was a huge rift between the copywriters and visualizers, part of the 'creative' groups and the support functions like finance, internal audit, etc. The hatred was mutual. The finance team disliked the fact that the agency seemed to have double standards while dealing with the creative team.

The creative teams would have people who would stroll in to the office around noon. Then have endless cups of coffee or surf the net. They would often start work when the people in the finance team would start leaving at the end of the day. The creative people hated the accountants for having no appreciation of the awards the campaign would win even if the account was not profitable. The accountants on the other hand would scorn these shabbily dressed artists and say that if the agency were left to them, they would go bankrupt before every month-end. This was a classic case of personality elements being suitable for a role and the organizational culture.

The personality elements of the people working in the creative departments of an agency are very different from those who are successful sales or finance people. The elements of personality that make someone creative are different from those that make someone analytical or become skilled at number crunching. That is why assessing these elements while hiring someone is necessary to ensure the right fit with the role as well as the organization's culture.

IDEAS

1. Assessing personality is important to see if the person is motivated to do what the role requires him to do. Wrong hires happen not because the person changed after getting the role, but because we did not uncover the aspect of personality and the derailers ahead of the decision. With no assessment done to find a fit between the person, the role and the culture of the organization, you may land up feeling that the person you interviewed is not the one who is working with you.
2. There is no such thing as 'good personality' or even 'bad'. There are no behaviours that any job could do with, for example, being sociable or being high on creativity. In some jobs, such as say that of an auditor, a highly creative person would be a misfit. Assessing these elements can help you take an informed decision.
3. The personality of the CEO and the leadership team has a tremendous impact on the work environment. When a CEO holds the HR or leadership team accountable for the poor scores on employee engagement or even on attrition, he does not see their personality of the selected individual as the reason for the problem. A senior leader is a role model for many. So make sure you assess her before letting her influence the culture of the organization.

9

Personality: The 'Bright Side'

HOGAN PERSONALITY INVENTORY

The Hogan Personality Inventory (HPI) is a tool that can be used to assess the candidate's personality to check for the extent of fit with the role. The results can be used to decide what developmental inputs the organization could provide the candidate in the early stages. The results could be useful indicators on proactive steps the organization can take to make the new leader successful. For example, if you know ahead of time that the person is strong in analysing data but is not someone who enjoys going out to influence the team, your decision may change.

I am a big fan of the HPI. I got certified in this a few years back and have been always amazed at the response of the leaders who have taken the inventory. They are always struck by the accuracy of what the inventory reveals about them. I have used the Leadership Forecast Series Report to coach several senior leaders and have found this to be the most insightful psychometric instrument that a practitioner could leverage. Yet it needs a person trained in the Hogan Suite to be able to make sense of the various terms and contextualize the jargon.

What was developed first in 1976 has undergone a number of revisions since. A million people in jobs have taken the HPI—from janitor to CEO. You could get a report called the Selection or Suitability Report, which you could use for selecting your leaders. This chapter is meant to simply tell you what a high or a low score could mean in the context of a senior-level hire. It tells us the fit between the person and the role.

The HPI is a measure of 'normal' personality. It was developed on normal people working in different roles in a variety of organizations. It is designed for use in selection, individualized assessment and career-related decision making. It provides detailed information regarding the 'bright' side of personality: *characteristics that facilitate or inhibit the person's ability to get along with others and to achieve his goals.*

The HPI has seven scales. In each scale there are sub-elements that I shall detail later. This is meant to be just a perspective of how this could help you make more informed decisions. Reading this book will not make you an expert on using the HPI. It will certainly make you aware of how to use assessment tools to hire your leaders. The scores are expressed in percentiles.

HPI scores above 65 per cent are high scores. Low scores are those below 35 per cent. HPI scores between 36 to 64 per cent are middle-range scores.

But the most important caveat to keep in mind is that the scale uses words that mean something different in everyday usage. So if someone has a low 'adjustment' score, it does not mean that the person will be unwilling to accommodate your needs. This term means something very different when used in the context of the Hogan scales. Getting a higher score is also not necessarily better than getting a lower one. We are now ready to explore the exciting world of personality assessment.

THE SEVEN SCALES OF HPI

The seven scales of Hogan Personality Inventory are discussed below:

Adjustment

This reflects the degree to which a person is calm and even-tempered or, conversely, moody and volatile. High adjustment people will appear confident, resilient and optimistic. Low scorers seem tense, irritable and negative. They worry about things long after the event is over. This tells us how a person deals with stress. High scorers deal better with stress than low scorers on this scale. High scorers tend to find it easier to bounce back from a setback. When given feedback, the high adjustment scorers tend to focus on the positive things said about them and quickly overlook the developmental gaps. The low adjustment scorers will lie awake at night going over the developmental opportunities over and over again, feeling overwhelmed until they fall asleep.

Ambition

This evaluates the degree to which a person seems leader-like, actively seeks status and values achievement.

People with high scores on ambition will come across as competitive and eager to advance. They enjoy winning and may be competitive even in situations when they do not need to. They are also vocal about their views. In meetings they are not hesitant to share their views and volunteer quickly to lead new initiatives or projects, especially, if it gives them a chance to put the spotlight upon themselves. Low scorers on ambition seem unassertive. They are less interested in advancement. They are happy working away in their office for years without craving to be recognized or given additional responsibility.

Sociability

This assesses the degree to which a person appears talkative and socially self-confident. High scorers seem outgoing, colourful and impulsive. They dislike working by themselves. High sociability people will be the ones to use the coffee breaks to get some face time with colleagues. These are people who will go out of the way to seek interactions with others. The buzz of people talking around them energizes them. This is exactly what can drive low sociability people to distraction. They need to not have to compulsively interact with co-workers. Low scorers seem reserved and quiet; they avoid calling attention to themselves and do not mind working alone.

Interpersonal Sensitivity

The scores on interpersonal sensitivity reflect social skill, tact and perceptiveness. It is no wonder that people who are popular display social skills and tact. That is why people with high scores on this element seem friendly, warm and popular. They are able to gauge the reaction of the audience to their message. They will modify their language to connect better with different individuals. They are able to display tact such that people can get the message without feeling hurt. Low scorers seem independent, frank and direct. They are comfortable delivering tough messages to people without flinching or mincing words.

Prudence

This tells us about the degree of self-control and conscientiousness. High scorers seem organized, dependable and thorough. They follow rules and are easy to supervise. These are the people who will not do anything that can be seen as challenging the norms in the workplace. They like fixed routines and structures. Low scorers on prudence may be viewed as impulsive and flexible. They tend to resist rules and feel suffocated if someone supervises them too closely. They may be creative and spontaneous for exactly the same reason. They resist being in a routine scenario and can be counted on to come up with creative ideas.

Inquisitive

The adjective that best describes people who score high on this scale is curious. This reflects the degree to which a person seems adventurous and imaginative. High scorers tend to be quick-witted and visionary, but they may be easily bored and not pay attention to details. They are the big-picture thinkers and strong in their strategic perspective. Low scorers tend to be practical, focused and able to concentrate for long periods. They are very good in finding ways of translating strategy into action. They will be the ones who will find practical ways to translate those ideas into an executable operating plan.

Learning Approach

This scale reflects the degree to which a person enjoys academic activities and values education as an end in itself. High scorers tend to enjoy reading and studying. They are likely to be tuned in to trends in the industry and be the first ones to sign up for a training programme or certification. Low scorers are less interested in formal education and more interested in hands-on learning on the job. They are impatient with theory and theoretical concepts. Low scorers find it difficult to enjoy reading and will not read unless they have no other option. In a workshop they are the people waiting for the class to end.

USING HPI FOR PERSON—ROLE FIT

The individual will be a mix of different kinds of scores on all these seven scales of HPI. When assessed on the seven scales the report will have some scores that are high, some that are medium and some low. It is also possible to have all scores in the high range or low range. The seven scales are all displayed in someone's Leadership Potential Profile.

CASE

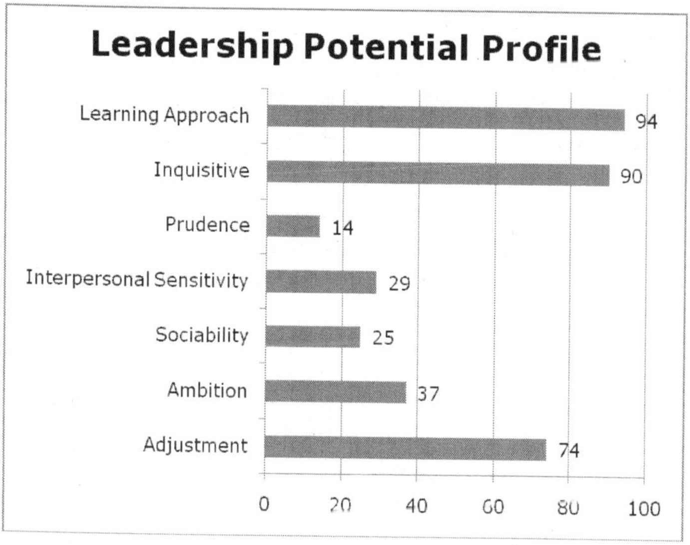

Interpretation

The high adjustment scores indicate that the person is confident, resilient and optimistic. The low scores on ambition and sociability show that he will be unassertive and less interested in advancement. He will appear reserved and quiet. He will not be the life of the office and will not mind working alone. The low prudence scores mean that this person is likely to be creative and spontaneous. While the person is likely to be a quiet worker, he may sometimes surprise you with his wit and sense of humour. You may even get some unusual and creative ideas from him. I would expect this person to be quick-witted and visionary given his high score on inquisitive scale. He may be easily bored with routine work and may not always pay attention to detail. I would also deduce that this person enjoys studying and learning new things.

I have simply used the description of the seven HPI scales based on whether the person's scores are high, low or average. Would you select this person? That depends on the kind of role you are hiring this leader for.

All personality elements have to be interpreted against a role. So, I would reframe the question and ask: For which role? I would look at the Success Profile[SM] of the role. Then ask if the person would be a strong fit or a moderate fit for the role. What would the role require the person to do to be successful? While there will rarely be situations that craft a role that matches the person's personality (and stays static), it is possible to keep some of the key elements in mind. Here is a sample analysis to find a fit:

> If the role is one that demands strong analytical skills and finding creative solutions to problems, this person will be a great fit. This person will also do well in a role that operates in a fast-paced and stressful environment and still remain unperturbed. This person will be comfortable with the kind of ambiguity and lack of structure that prevails in many start-ups. He will be quick to adjust to the demands of an unfolding environment (high adjustment).
>
> He seems confident and willing to take charge of a group or project when necessary, but he is equally comfortable letting others take a lead role. The person would do well in a role that gives him 'alone time'. He values privacy and may prefer to communicate in writing

rather than face-to-face. If the role requires the person to be constantly communicating with large teams he may occasionally say things which may cause controversy or concern (low sociability).

Such a leader won't mind taking unpopular positions, enforcing standards or pushing people for results (low interpersonal sensitivity).

Does the role require someone who is a big-picture thinker or one who gets into operational details? Is the role about managing innovation or devising a strategy to launch a new product? This person will be visionary and can think quickly on his feet, generate lots of ideas and will be curious about how things work. He will be creative but easily bored with the details of implementation (high inquisitive).

Does the role require someone who has to stay abreast of technological changes or changes in the regulatory environment? He would be really good at that. Colleagues may think of him as bright and well-informed. Some others may think he likes to show off his knowledge (high learning approach).

CASE

The role is that of a CEO of CotonFabrique, a billion-Euro textile firm headquartered in Paris. Of late their major competitor has also entered India and the market is witnessing small local players launch new designs. CotonFabrique has lost a number of scientists and designers. Rising attrition numbers is a major concern. The firm has to keep pace with all the innovations that the competitor has introduced. The media keeps speculating whether CotonFabrique will eventually pull out of India if they see a few more quarters of sluggish growth. You are on the panel that has to choose between two candidates, each with successful track records: Atul and Manish. Their HPI reports are given below. Who would you choose as the CEO of the firm?

I will make some assumptions about what the Success Profile℠ would define as the critical elements of the role. One of the big tasks of the new CEO would be to craft a vision for the company that hinges on bringing innovative products into the marketplace. So the role needs someone who can be a visionary and strategic thinker.

To stem attrition, the CEO has to assure the employees that CotonFabrique will win in the marketplace and will have to show a few quick wins. It needs someone who can work with the employees and assure the media that the company is on the upswing.

Compare the HPI profiles of Atul and Manish. Both have some striking similarities in the HPI scores. They are high on ambition. Manish has high adjustment scores while Atul is low on adjustment. These high scores imply that Manish will appear much more in charge and confident. He will bring in a dose of optimism in the organization. This is what the employees need to start rebuilding the organization. Manish is lower on sociability than Atul. While Atul will be more comfortable meeting people, his cautious approach (high prudence) will soon dampen the enthusiasm for trying out any innovative ideas the employees may have had. Manish is creative and has many ideas and will probably be able to garner support in small groups. Both are unlikely to value training and development for the staff (low learning approach). This may prove to be a barrier as innovation is a key need of the business if they have to succeed in the long run.

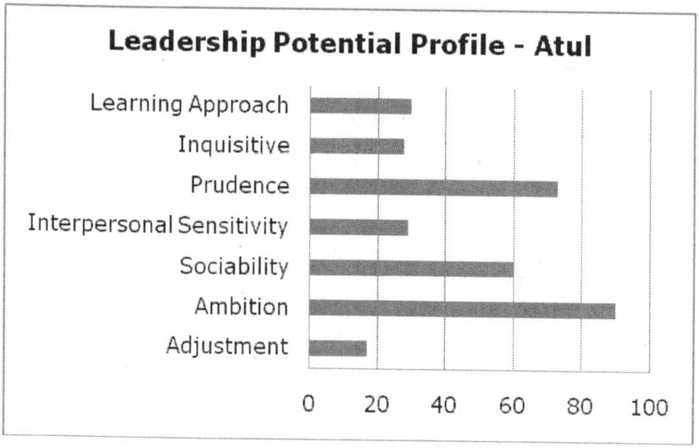

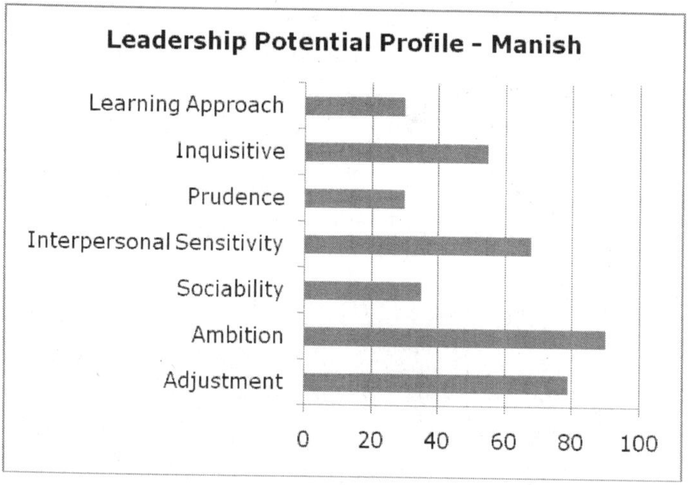

If one had to find a better fit with the demands of the role, I would opt for Manish. Manish is more likely to succeed given the demands of the role as envisaged in the Success Profile^{SM}. He could work with a coach to learn how to fulfil his development needs.

IDEAS

1. To create a fit between the person and the role, first understand the enabling behaviours that facilitate success in the role. Then assess the personality elements to find the role–person fit. You need to use the right psychometric tool to measure aspects of personality that will play a big part in the fit of the individual with the role. The Hogan Personality Inventory is a great tool to be used for selection decisions. The basis for selecting or rejecting a candidate at the top has to lie in the extent of fit between the demands of the role and the personality fit. The better the fit, the more successful the person will be.
2. There is no such thing as 'good personality' or 'bad personality'. There will be elements of personality that will enable the person to do what the role needs him to do to succeed. The same person could succeed or fail in another role or even when she is doing the same role in another organization.
3. Someone who has been very successful in the same role in the past could now be facing rapidly sliding performance. That could happen because the external environment of the business has changed and what is now needed to succeed has less fit with the person's personality.

10

Personality: The 'Dark Side'

HOGAN DEVELOPMENT SURVEY

We all like to put our best foot forward while dealing with others. The job interview is a perfect example of such an interaction when the candidate is trying to put himself across as one having many positive attributes. This is impression management at its best. It can be as simple as smiling warmly at the interviewer, to demonstrating friendliness and being seen as an extrovert by speaking to others and behaving in a manner that will show them in positive light. Most people like to show that they are really skillful in handling people are hard-working, organized, plan well yet spontaneous (can there be such a thing?) and of course they can take decisions with just the oh-so-correct mix of head and heart.

So it is important not to depend on clichéd questions such as 'So tell me about yourself.' Or 'Tell me about your strengths and development needs.' We squirm about using the word weaknesses because candidates, especially potential employees, do not have weaknesses. They all have 'development needs'. This is actually how the interviewers return the favour of massive levels of impression management being done by candidates.

My suggestion is that you should not depend on untrained people asking such naive questions to understand the personality derailers the person has. The HPI gives us a view of the 'bright side'. The performance risks or derailers make up the 'dark side' of the personality. I recommend using the Hogan Development Survey (HDS) that has eleven performance risks that interfere with a person's ability to build relationships with others and create good cohesive teams. These counterproductive behaviours are known to have ruined many a corporate leader's career. These derailers will show up when a person is not actively managing his public image.

The common occasions when a derailer shows up could be in situations of high stress or change, multi-tasking, when a person is overworked or any time when the person lets down his guard and relaxes. Think of the times when someone cracks a joke that is completely inappropriate even though he is among friends. That is because a derailer will show up whenever we are not actively managing our public image.

A poor job fit causes a lot of stress. Hiring the wrong person in a senior role causes enough stress to make the leader's derailers affect daily behaviour. Some of these lapses can be crucial. A strength that has been overused becomes a derailer. While taking the opinions of peers is a good idea, the same behaviour can be a derailer when the leader is unable to take a decision until she reaches a consensus. After all, when everyone agrees to a decision, it lowers the risk of one person being blamed in case of failure. The good news is that self-awareness obtained through HDS coupled with strong development efforts can reduce the impact of the risks associated with high scores.

We have seen that HPI gives us scores on seven personality elements that could be enablers or barriers in a role. A high score on prudence will enable a person to succeed in a role that demands conformity to rules and procedures. An air traffic controller's job would demand a person who can be very comfortable following a well-established routine that would be hard for a person with low prudence to perform. A low prudence score would be an advantage in a job that demands creativity and thinking out of the box.

The HDS is not job-specific. These counterproductive behaviours are exhibited whenever a person is not paying attention to his public image. Higher scores on HDS increase the chances that derailers will be more problematic for that performance risk.

Scores more than the ninetieth percentile indicate that there is a high risk of the derailer affecting the person's behaviour. Scores between the seventieth and eighty-ninth percentile are considered moderate-risk. Scores between the fortieth and sixty-ninth percentile are considered low-risk. Scores less than the thirty-ninth percentile are no risk. Almost everyone has one or two scores approaching the high range. Three or more high risks make the behaviour problematic. In periods of high stress, such as, during the early days of being in a new job, or after joining a new company, the stress of having to prove himself quickly will increase the probability of the derailers affecting the behaviour.

Derailers are deeply ingrained personality traits that affect leadership style and action. Leaders get insulated from feedback that is uncomfortable for them. When a person begins to get away with his faults, the person sees no need to manage the public image. Then the derailers go unchecked and lead to the end of many a brilliant career. When a leader who is very competent displays his temper in meetings, very often the team has to reluctantly look the other way. This unchecked behaviour will lead to an unpleasant display on an important occasion and abruptly end the person's career.

THE ELEVEN SCALES OF HDS

The Hogan Development Survey has eleven scales. Each one of them is discussed with the help of case studies:

Excitable

A person with a high-risk score in this scale will come across as one who has sharp mood swings, hot tempered, easily irritated, unpredictable and hard to please. People with high risk on this scale deal with stress by abruptly quitting or ending relationships or tasks. They do not persist through the ups and downs of a project or a relationship. They might be overly enthusiastic about people or projects and then suddenly become disappointed with them. They will have favourites for a few days or months and then one fine day for a trivial reason the favourite colleague will fall from favour.

CASE

Hardev Singh is the CEO of a major paint company. He was such a terror in the office that even the slight hesitation in answering his questions could lead to Hardev yelling and insulting the person. His secretary's job was to give a 'weather report' to the person who was going in for a meeting with Hardev. He was feared for his mercurial temper and violent mood swings. Many a colleague who came in with bad news would go back without meeting Hardev if his secretary said that the boss was in a foul mood. 'Praise makes people slacken up', said Hardev. 'I am a demanding boss but it is hard to keep my cool with such incompetent people around. They cannot even articulate their ideas without fumbling and stammering.' Hardev's subordinates have to keep guessing which company-wide initiative is the flavour of the season. Every time Hardev hears of an idea from someone who is high on the popularity charts, a new initiative is launched. Last year for one quarter everyone was focused on 'Win the Customer'. That slogan changed the next month to 'Happy Employees Happy Customers'. This month there are posters that encourage everyone to 'Winnovate', i.e., innovate to win. They are trying to guess what the next slogan will be. Hardev feels people do not think through the execution plans of these initiatives. That's why he has had to drop them and find something that works.

Sceptical

People with high-risk scores on this scale will be argumentative. They are the ones who are most likely to read the fine print of a contract word by word before signing on the dotted line. Since they are socially insightful, they are the first ones to sniff out organizational politics and coteries of power. Their cynicism makes them often see plots aimed at marginalizing their ideas or work where none exist. If criticized they may react sharply and complain about being offended. They worry about being discriminated, sometimes on grounds that are imaginary. Their protests may be disproportionate compared to the criticism being offered. This behaviour will lead to colleagues becoming more guarded in what they say in their presence for fear of being chastised. They mistrust others' intentions, are alert for signs of mistreatment and then will challenge or blame others when it seems to occur. As a result, a leader with high-risk scores on the sceptical scale, seems to lack trust.

CASE

George is the head of HR in a major airline. He managed a large team of experienced HR professionals. His direct reportees would feel frustrated about George's cynicism and inability to trust them in any way.

George would announce to his team that he would be away on travel and then come back a day early just to check if his team was slacking off because he was gone. Whenever someone brings in a report, he asks another team member to secretly cross-check the figures. He once ran into three of his team members at a bar in the city. Since then he has been trying to find out if this 'clique' was plotting to complain about their work-load.

Last year when a team member told George about a strike by the pilots that was brewing, he asked a dozen people to verify the rumour and the possibility of the strike taking place. Anyone who came to him with any information would be subjected to hours of grilling and cross-questions that would exasperate the person who would swear never to volunteer any information in future.

His team members say that George did not trust his own shadow. So one couldn't really expect him to trust his team. George's peers would say that he would smell evil designs when there were none. Even light-hearted banter between friends would be analysed by George for possible hidden messages and plots. At the office party, in the presence of George all jokes and light hearted jibes would come to a grinding halt. The colleagues never know what he will take offence to. When they suddenly go quiet in his presence, George is convinced that the group was complaining about him behind his back. Why else did they suddenly stop?

Cautious

People in the high-risk zone on this scale are risk-averse. They worry about the consequence of failure. This fear of failures comes from their overly worrying about being criticized. They are deeply concerned about making mistakes or being embarrassed. They are always looking for a risk-free decision especially if there is a lot at stake. In trying to safeguard against all kinds of possibilities they lose precious time. A leader who has very high-risk scores on this element could ask for multiple options and spend time doing the risk analysis of each one. I suspect, they are the ones who buy all possible kinds of insurance policies to cover every possibility. At times of stress, they will become defensive and extremely conservative. As a result, a leader with high-risk scores on cautious seems resistant to change and reluctant to take chances. In an industry where a firm's survival depends on taking a quick decision there are chances of moderate to calculated risks. In the case of Gary, his derailer cost the company irreversible losses.

CASE

Gary is head of the legal division for a major chocolate manufacturer. One of the batches of chocolates was found to have fungus. While the claim was being analysed through lab tests, the competitor launched a campaign that clearly attacked the quality of Gary's product. There was an outrage among the employees. They felt that Gary should file a suit against the competitor's claims and give the court the results of laboratory tests that would build consumer awareness against the campaign. When the media asked Gary how he would respond to the competitor's campaign, he simply said, 'No comments.' He believed that it was a temporary blip that would die a natural death. The inactivity cost the company some loss of market share. Gary's colleague, the head of sales, expressed his anguish over the loss and said that they should immediately counter the claim.

The company steadily lost market share every month. When asked for a way to stop the competitor, Gary retracted into his shell and read up every case that had a similar scenario to tackle. The opinion was divided. In some cases the courts had taken a sympathetic stance. In others they had let the offender off with a relatively minor fine. Gary then prepared a major position paper that clearly weighed the pros and cons of taking such a stance. The CEO asked Gary what he would recommend. Gary asked for more time. The CEO was furious at having lost so much time and market share. Gary sought the opinion of every senior legal counsel he knew. Their opinion too was divided. That did not help. After losing market share for seven months and with no clear recommendation from Gary, the CEO decided to take the competitor to court. Gary kept warning the CEO that this was not a risk-free option. Everyone was surprised when the competitor meekly stopped the campaign without a fight. Gary's company had lost 11 per cent of the market share during this time and a drop to the second position in market share.

Reserved

People in the high-risk zone of this derailer often come across as uncommunicative. Their natural tendency is not to have face to face meetings unless it is inevitable. They are therefore more comfortable dealing with their teams through email or through very short meetings. When the whole team decides to go out for lunch, she will announce that she prefers to grab a sandwich at her desk so that she could finish her work and go home early. On a long transcontinental flight with a colleague, she would rather catch up on sleep than speak to her co-passenger. She explained her position by saying, 'I can always speak to him in the office if I need to. There are so many movies to watch on a flight.' They appear independent, uncaring, aloof and uncomfortable with strangers. When stressed, they deal with this situation by withdrawing and being uncommunicative. They are often accused of lacking interest in or awareness of the feelings of others. As a result leader with high-risk scores on reserved are poor communicators.

CASE

Mehernosh was great at his work. He was not a social person. He was a man of few words, ate lunch alone in his office while reading the newspaper and avoided office parties. His communication with the employees was through email, with which he was very regular. He used to send out a 'Daily Snapshot' to keep employees posted and used to feel irritated when people would ask the same question that he had answered in the previous day's email. People still talk about how he snubbed an employee who wanted to seek a clarification on the incentive scheme. 'There was an email sent this morning which explains the scheme in detail. I expect to employ literate people in the organization. By that I mean someone who knows how to read emails. Don't expect me to spoon feed you with all the information.' His pet peeve was that no one read their e-mails. When asked if he would fund a party to celebrate a successful sales quarter, he said that he did not mind funding any number of parties as long as he did not have to attend them. When one of his colleagues lost his wife in a freak accident, the whole office went over to convey their condolences, except for Mehernosh. At the funeral, everyone commented about his insensitivity. Mehernosh said that a funeral was a time when people want privacy. A funeral is not an excuse to socialize, he said.

Leisurely

People in the high-risk zone of this derailer often come across as being quick to volunteer for a task and then come up with a series of excuses for not doing it. They like to be independent, often ignoring others' requests and becoming irritable if they persist. They want to work at their own pace and standards and feel burdened when asked to work faster or differently. If pressurized by others to agree on a method that is different from what he had proposed, he will keep arguing in favour of his approach until his colleagues give in. If the colleagues insist on going by the approach that the majority had recommended, he will figure out a way of either adopting his own approach anyway or not doing the task at all. As a result, a leader with high-risk scores on leisurely will come across as stubborn, procrastinative and uncooperative.

CASE

Dr Joshi (popularly called 'Doc') is the head of research with a large generic drug manufacturer. He is always at loggerheads with his peers. In the weekly meeting of the leadership team, very often he will hijack the entire meeting by arguing with every idea that has not been suggested by him. He will preface it by saying, 'I think it is a great idea but ...' His peers feel upset that for every decision, Doc can single handedly sabotage it by his endless resistance. When the peers sought the help of the CEO to veto his objection to a project, Doc sulked for days and stopped attending meetings. That delayed things even more. Finally they gave in to Doc's idea in sheer despair.

Doc wants to be involved in every committee or group formed at the leadership level. Otherwise he will complain loudly about it in the meetings about the company ignoring scientists or more specifically, the R&D function. When invited, he will rarely attend the group's meetings. He does not confirm his presence or absence till the last minute, making it hard for the others to plan. If someone calls him up to remind him, Dr Joshi will complain about being flooded with work and narrate his numerous real and imaginary health problems for a long time. The call would end by Doc chastising the caller on the phone for disturbing his busy schedule. Dr Joshi is always falling behind every project and misses most of his deadlines. He blames it on being understaffed.

Bold

People in the high-risk zone of this scale come across as arrogant. They are prone to making exaggerated promises and committing to outcomes which others may cringe to sign up for. They have the tendency to over-evaluate their talents, not admit mistakes or take anyone's advice. Under pressure, they will bluster and bluff. They have a reputation for having inflated views of their competency and worth. During a feedback session with a senior leader, he told me, 'The 360 degree feedback was very effective in capturing the various strengths that I have. However, I am not sure that the instrument is capable of identifying the developmental gaps just as well.' Most of them will state that any success of the team or the organization is clearly due to their contribution. Failures are either explained away or blamed on others. They enjoy announcing their stretch targets with huge fanfare. As a result, a leader with high-risk scores on bold seems unable to admit mistakes or learn from experience.

CASE

Kiran has taken over as the COO of a fast-food chain. On the first day while he was addressing the employees, he told them, 'All those who miss their quarterly targets would have to look for jobs with the competitor.' He then added that joining the competitor may be the best thing the poor performers could do for the company.

The HR head stared at him in disbelief as he stared at the series of text messages on his phone from angry employees.

Kiran also announced a consolidation of franchisees under four new vice-presidents in the same meeting. This was news even to the senior leaders who were caught totally off-guard. That meant big changes to be made in the organization structure.

When the employees asked him why this change was being made, Kiran laughed loudly and said that he needed to shake up people in the company who were used to a 'sleepy, take-it-easy culture'. When the performance results looked up after a quarter, Kiran ascribed this to the 'kick-ass culture' he was fostering. The employees felt that he overestimated his contributions and was closed to feedback. When he lost three of the four new vice-presidents in three months, Kiran said that they were unable to take the heat and get used to the new pace. Eighteen months later, the company was worse off than what it was before Kiran took charge. When asked by the press, he said he understood the nuances of this business more than anyone else. But for the changes he had made, the company would have been worse off.

Mischievous

Leaders with scores that put them in the high-risk area on the mischievous scale are impulsive. They are socially adept and charming. They create extremely positive impressions during interviews in person since it is easy for them to give witty responses to the interviewer's questions. This makes the interviewers believe that the person is a quick learner and confident enough to learn what he does not know. Their style of leadership is charismatic. They are comfortable taking risks, forever ready to challenge status quo and test limits. They make hasty decisions because of their impulsive nature. This often leads them to overlook information or early signals resulting in errors. They do not enjoy reflecting on what went wrong and hence do not learn from experience. When confronted with their errors or poor results, they move on. They like to be seen as risk takers and seek excitement. As a result, a leader with high-risk scores on mischievous may seem to have trouble maintaining commitments and staying the course over time.

CASE

Sohail leads the information technology practice in a consultancy firm. He is charming and witty and is the life of the party. His spontaneous repartees and limericks can keep everyone in splits. He is well travelled, suave and certainly charismatic. His team of followers thinks they have a manager who can do no wrong. He is always everyone's choice to be the host of the entertainment show that employees annually put up. The show is attended by every employee and their spouse. When Sohail mimicked the CEO's walk and accented speech, everyone laughed. The CEO pretended to be a good sport and played along. The next day Sohail was called to his office and told that a senior executive was expected to know where to draw the line.

Sohail has been often been told that his spontaneity can be a liability in a business scenario. He got the financials wrong when he committed to a new client the firm had pursued for a while. When the CEO told him that the firm would make significant losses, he simply shrugged his shoulders and said that the error assured him that he was still human. 'To err is human.' he said to the CEO, 'when you forgive me, it will be divine.' Sohail said that he needed to take risks and took a spontaneous call. The CEO said that the new business would be unviable unless the financials were renegotiated.

Colourful

Leaders with scores that put them in the high-risk area on the colourful scale are very high on their need for attention. They will be the first ones to try out a new hairstyle or the latest in fashion. They enjoy the fact that others keep speculating what they will do next that is a novelty. They try to be dramatic, engaging and attention-seeking. They can come across as talented and interesting, but ignoring other's requests. When stressed they deal with it by becoming very busy. The leader with high-risk scores on colourful seems preoccupied with being noticed and may lack sustained focus. They are usually so preoccupied with being noticed that they do not realize that their team members need attention too.

CASE

People cannot help noticing how clever Rohit is. He is clever, interesting and expressive. He changes his hairstyle every now and then. For a while he had long flowing hair. Then one morning he showed up with his head shaven. Many colleagues find him very flashy. When he came back from vacation last year, he showed everyone the tattoo of Harley Davidson that he had got.

He can always be counted on to handle the media when they come to interview him about the slipping bottom line. He made a strong first impression even with the board with his dramatic presentation where he had got a magician to demonstrate how the margins were vanishing. People have not forgotten how the magician made a large pile of coins disappear from the table without even touching them. The joke now is that maybe if Rohit made an effort to get into the details, the coins would not disappear so rapidly. He does not have a clearly designated successor because he has had a lot of attrition among his direct reportees. They claim that Rohit enjoys hogging the limelight so much that he does not have time to coach and train anyone else. When he read the comments in his 360 degree feedback report, he was shocked with the comments from his team. He thought several comments about him being narcissistic were unfair.

Imaginative

Leaders with scores that put them in the high-risk area on the imaginative scale are eccentric and highly creative at the same time. They do not just display their creativity while solving a problem. They live their life in an unconventional manner. When stressed they become unpredictable and act in a manner that seem eccentric, creative and sometimes unusual. They enjoy being labeled as unpredictable. The result is that a leader with high-risk scores on imaginative seems creative but possibly lacking in judgement.

CASE

Kelly heads one of the largest advertising and public relations agencies. His presentations are always much awaited in any conference. He always has an interpretation that is a clutter-breaker. Although he is fun to work with, he is easily distracted and communicates in unpredictable, idiosyncratic, or confusing ways.

Kelly's office has been photographed by several magazines

and features frequently when he is being photographed for the celebrities' page in the newspaper. He has an office wall full of photos with every possible film star and business leader. You cannot miss the life-size photograph displayed in his office that shows Kelly clutching his award at the Cannes Film Festival with a smattering of Hollywood actors. Kelly has a large aquarium in his office with piranhas. The large grey African parrot in the corner of Kelly's office occasionally startles visitors who are meeting him for the first time.

Kelly is the reason why the agency has won several clients who swear by his work. He is also the reason that the same clients have dropped him. He created the most memorable campaigns for the most mundane products. He kept the director of marketing of the biggest steel producer of the country waiting in his office as he completed his daily routine of fifteen minutes of tai-chi exercises. Kelly said he was building his concentration so that he could listen to the 'soul of the idea'.

Diligent

Leaders with scores that put them in the high-risk area on the diligent scale are perfectionists. They set high standards of performance for themselves and others. They work hard and will ensure that everyone around does the same. They are usually believers not just in the quality of work, but also the sheer quantity of it. They are overly concerned about being meticulous and precise. Sometimes they will follow a rule to its letter and create absurd situations for others. They may come across as picky, critical and stubborn when under pressure. They are conscientious and hard to please. A leader with high-risk scores on this scale finds it hard to empower his team members. Kannan is a great example of someone whose derailer is diligent.

CASE

Kannan says he is a perfectionist. He says that it is infuriating to find how shabby and careless people are when it comes to writing reports and preparing presentations. If the font sizes used in the presentation are not as per the company's official template he will not read it until the person makes the change. He will spend hours debating on the precise wording of a slide. The team members dread his behaviour before any review with the board. Everyone will have to reword a slide several times before Kannan gives his approval. For a week before the review, the team works till the wee hours of the morning. The joke is that it took Michelangelo less time to paint the ceiling of the Sistine Chapel.

His subordinates wish he would empower them without micromanaging them constantly. Kannan works late. He has not taken his complete vacation days in any year. He complains that every time he plans his vacation, there is some crisis in the office that forces him to drop the plans or come back halfway through the holiday. He is annoyed that his team does not share the same work ethic. When the company announced a work-from-home option Kannan announced loudly in his team meeting that the policy did not apply to his 'part of the planet'.

All his team members work on weekends. Kannan will negotiate hard with them when they ask for vacation days. The team members know that to get a week's vacation they need to ask for much more so that Kannan has the satisfaction of cutting short their plans.

Dutiful

Being approval dependent is the fatal flaw of leaders with scores in the high-risk area on the dutiful scale. They come across as eager to please anyone in authority and reluctant to act independently. For every little decision, they will spend hours trying to interpret what their manager would approve of. They are keen on being seen as cordial and agreeable and are always eager to please. When asked why they do not exercise their own judgement, they will state that if everyone were to follow that philosophy, anarchy would prevail. When stressed they are reluctant to take independent action and conform. A leader with high-risk scores on dutiful tends to be pleasant and agreeable, but reluctant to support subordinates.

CASE

Madhav was always eager to please—not just the boss, but everyone else. He had the reputation of being a 'yes-man'. He has a weekly meeting with the CEO to keep him posted on the upcoming decisions. The CEO had told him initially that as the head of sales, Madhav could approve the expenses that fall within the financial authority guidelines issued by the finance department without keeping the CEO informed. Madhav, however, continues to bring every little decision to the weekly meeting. Of late, the CEO uses this meeting to catch up on his emails while Madhav drones on about every piece of trivia.

His team hates the Budgets & Forecast meetings. It was the same charade every year. The team would put together a sales forecast for the year which would be a stretch target anyway. Madhav would present the numbers to the CEO and come back having agreed to a substantially higher target. The team would do a mental calculation and know that they were unlikely to make any sales incentives with the targets being so unreasonable. The reverse was true when it came to their budgets. No matter what the team budgets, Madhav will agree to a huge drop in the budget once he meets the CEO. The team refers to him as 'His Master's Voice' when they catch up informally. Madhav knows about this moniker and is quite proud of it. So his team has learnt to inflate the estimates so that they have a reasonable chance of achieving their sales targets. When the team complained, he would agree that the revised target and budgets were unreasonable, but said that he was helpless against the powers that be. During discussions with the CEO, Madhav agreed that it would stretch the team to take on stiffer targets and smaller budgets. Of late he has taken up playing golf simply because the new CEO is crazy about it.

INTERPRETING THE DARK SIDE

Now we will discuss some case histories to understand how to interpret the high-risk and medium-risk derailers from a HDS report.

CASE 1

Here are the scores for a leader's Hogan Development Survey. We know that HDS scores that are more than the ninetieth percentiles are in the high-risk of affecting the individual's reputation during moments of stress or relaxation. Scores between the seventieth and eighty-ninth percentiles are considered moderate-risk. See the Leadership Challenge Forecast below. Using this definition we can say that the high-risk derailers for this individual are excitable

(90) and reserved (93). The moderate-risk area is cautious (79). It is common for everyone to have one or two derailers. This is the dark side of personality that has to be actively managed to not show up at times of high stress. Leadership roles are stressful. The leader is constantly under scrutiny from the employees, the shareholders, the regulators and the media. Without awareness of the derailers through structured assessment and feedback, an otherwise capable leader may fall victim to the derailers.

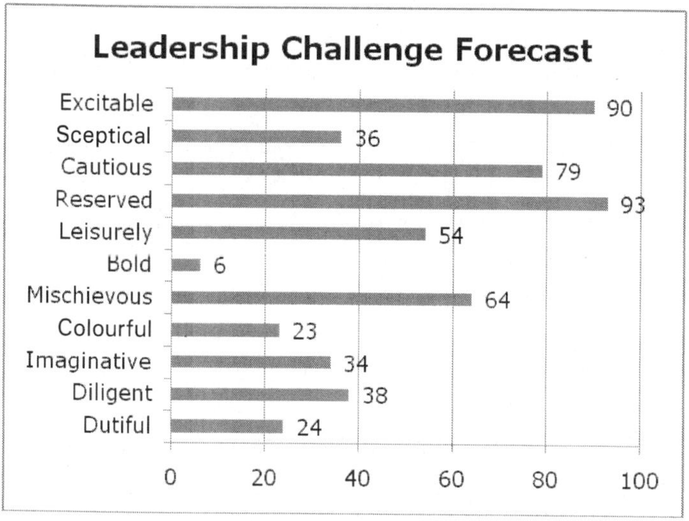

This person's Leadership Challenge Report gives us a view of his derailers using the HDS scales. The high excitable scores tell us that he is likely to swing between extremes from being really pleasant to hysterical without any warning. High reserved scores warn us that at times when there is a crisis there is a high probability that the leader may withdraw into his shell and not be available to his team. High periods of stress will also get reflected in mood swings as shown by his high scores on excitable. When this person is stressed, people will not be able to anticipate his reaction. Such behaviour will make the team very apprehensive in giving him any piece of news that may trigger off the excitable derailer. That may make it hard for the leader to get an early warning from a colleague about a brewing catastrophe. In many scenarios the leader would not know of a problem until it is too late. His team members would not be forthcoming in giving their opinions, especially when there is bad news. A visit to his office would be preceded by a short stop in his secretary's office to inquire, 'What is the boss's mood like today?' People will tell him what he wants to hear. Many meetings may start with humour and his pulling someone's leg and will often be about the person wanting more and more data (moderate-risk score on cautious) until something will trigger off the mood swing. He may become upset by unexpected demands and may say things that he may regret later.

A common corridor conversation after the meeting will be, 'He seemed to be in such a good mood until... Wonder what triggered it off?' The high score on cautious indicates that he dislikes making mistakes and being criticized. He may tend to watch his team closely to ensure that they too get things right. Doing so may undermine their confidence. He may also be slow to make decisions, which could frustrate an action-oriented staff.

CASE 2

Here is the profile of another leader. What do you see as the key derailers?

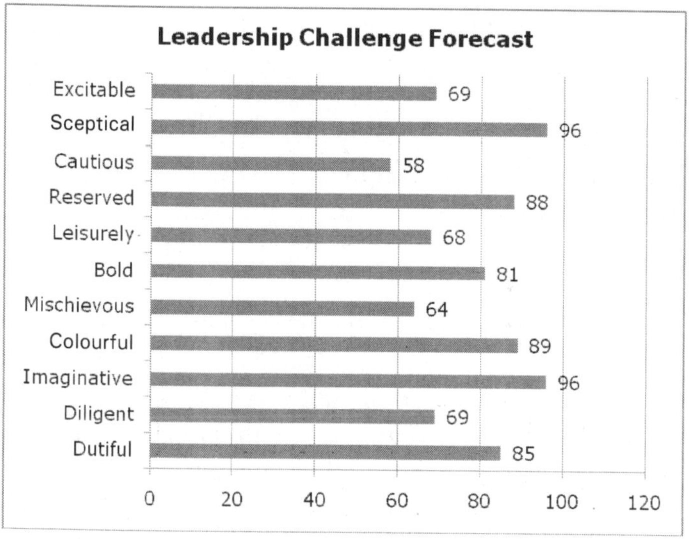

Remember that derailers are strengths that are being overused. A perfect example of this would be the top two derailers, sceptical and imaginative. Both are in the ninety-sixth percentile.

Leaders with high-risk scores on sceptical would be socially skilled and perceptive and have an instinctive ability to fathom organizational politics. A high-risk score on sceptical means that this leader would also find it hard to trust her co-workers. She will have a tendency to be suspicious and argumentative which others will perceive as being difficult and uncooperative. Because this leader finds it hard to trust colleagues, she will see motives when none exists. So when colleagues give her suggestions to improve, she is likely to overreact to perceived threats and become argumentative when she feels slighted and take critical feedback personally.

You may recall, the imaginative scale concerns thinking and acting in interesting, unusual and even eccentric ways. High-risk scores on this scale show that this leader is very creative but possibly lacking in judgement. Her colleagues will appreciate her creativity and spontaneity. She will also bring in strategic and visionary thinking which an organization can leverage. On the other hand, her playfulness, occasionally lapsing into idiosyncratic communicative style such as using phrases that make no sense to others and her unusual ideas may detract from her credibility. If in her role she has to handle the media, she may have to be briefed to stay with the scripted responses or else she may possibly land up making statements that leaves everyone red-faced. When given this feedback, she will view it as an attempt by 'the opposition' to underplay her success because they are jealous.

In addition, this leader has some other derailers too that are in the moderate-risk zone. Moderate-risk scores on reserved show that this leader will sporadically come across as indifferent to the feelings of others, almost seeming aloof. When stressed she will stop communicating with others. So, they will view her as an 'absent leader' even when the leader believes they are fully engaged.

Moderate scores on bold show that this person will come across as confident and carry deep convictions. She may not care too much about the opinion of others. Her style of being very direct with others while giving feedback may sometimes lead to hurt team members. Her manager would find that she may not listen attentively to feedback about her own performance. She may have trouble learning from her mistakes.

Moderate-risk on the colourful scale means that this person will seem clever, interesting and expressive and make a strong first impression. She would charm most potential interviewers with her wit and creative ideas but may not go forth on detailed execution plans. In team meetings she will usually be a high-profile participant, sometimes be long-winded in speaking but may not actively listen to others.

Moderate-risk scores on the diligent scale shows that this leader may occasionally focus more on getting along with her boss in times of stress than getting along with her staff, which can erode her credibility with the subordinates. She probably prefers to avoid conflict and confrontations and may be uncomfortable giving others negative feedback.

UNUSUAL WAYS OF ASSESSING LEADERSHIP TALENT

We hear of companies or various institutions using unusual methods of hiring leaders. In his book *The Rare Find: Spotting Exceptional Talent Before Everyone Else,* George Anders talks about how the US Army hires.

> The US Army's Special Forces size up candidates in a nineteen-day selection process in which no bullets are fired. The army isn't looking for the world's best shooters; it can teach that. What it wants are resilient soldiers who can tackle unpredictable challenges. One test is to ask a group of prospects to move a trailer that's missing a wheel to a point two and a half mile away. The soldiers have some pipes, rope and other objects at their disposal. The bare axle can never touch the ground. What they don't know is that there isn't a good way

> to put the elements together to get it done. A sergeant watches not to find who has the best solution but who best handles the fact that there is no answer. The winning candidates may not be honours graduates of West Point, but they have the grit that can pay off in tough, isolated assignments overseas.

They have clearly identified a method of simulating a high-stress scenario to bring up enablers and derailers in that role. The army has identified the workplace scenario of these officers as VUCA, an acronym for volatile, uncertain, complex and ambiguous. 'What it wants are resilient soldiers who can tackle unpredictable challenges.' They believe that the officers they hire must demonstrate an ability to succeed in this environment. So their assessment simulates this scenario. The exercise shows how the officers accomplish these demanding tasks against impossible deadlines. The entire selection goes beyond the CV and focuses on 'grit' and resilience as the two personality factors that will enable success. The stress will show the derailers. It is a good hiring process. (Anders, 2011)

Should you then select leaders by having them move a trailer that's missing a wheel over a two-and-a-half mile distance? No. The reason why this method works for the army is that the method of assessment simulates the nature of the job they will do. So the assessment exercise actually shows how a candidate would react in the real world when he actually is in a similar situation.

DDI has discovered that organizations with the most effective hiring policies were more likely to use the following four practices (Inc Magazine):

- Job interviews in which candidates are asked to describe specific examples of their skills,
- Automated CV screening and search,
- Assessments that predict whether candidates are motivated by the factors associated with a particular job or a company's values and ways of doing things, and
- Simulations that gauge specific job-related abilities and skills.

IDEAS

1. At senior levels, we rarely have leaders who have a competency problem to be successful in doing the job. They fail inevitably because of the derailers that make up the 'dark side' of personality. The Hogan Development Survey (HDS) can give us powerful insights about the derailers that will show up in the leader when he is not actively managing his public image. Each derailer also has a positive side to it as well. Usually in a selection interview what is likely to come through is the positive side of a derailer which may be in the high-risk zone. A high-risk leader on the bold scale will impress the panel with his confidence. It will be difficult for them to know that this person will not learn from his mistakes or even listen to feedback about his performance.
2. There is no such thing as 'good personality' or 'bad personality'. There will be elements of personality that will enable the person to do what the role needs him to do to succeed. The same person could succeed or fail in another role or even when he is doing the same role in another organization.
3. The hiring assessment need not be only psychometric assessments. In the case of the US Army, a group of trained psychologists gather data during the nineteen-day selection process. I am not aware of any corporation that hires its leaders using such a long process. Assessments can be in many forms. They need to simulate the key personality elements that will be the difference between great and average performance. Just doing an interview to find a mental fit with the job may not be enough. It needs to be assessed using the right psychometric tool. You cannot measure blood pressure by using a compass.

SECTION
3

11

Organizational Fit

Values and Motivations

Hogan measures personality along three dimensions: the 'bright-side' of personality, the 'dark-side' of personality and values. The bright side of personality, measured by the Hogan Personality Inventory (HPI), is the characteristics that people exhibit when at their best. The dark side of personality, measured by the Hogan Development Survey (HDS), is made up of strengths that, under stress or boredom, become debilitating obstacles to building and maintaining productive relationships. Values—measured by the Motives, Values and Preferences Inventory (MVPI)—are the core beliefs, drivers and interests that drive behaviour. Values are a powerful, inherent part of your personality that shape the choices that you make.

The values that leaders hold are important indicators of the culture that they create in the organizations they lead. A person's core values and goals and the activities that he enjoys, give meaning to his life. These values, goals and activities are part of a person's identity. Consequently, they are a person's key drivers. They are what a person desires and strives to attain.

In addition, people prefer to work with others who share their values, dislike those who do not and are happiest working in environments that are consistent with their values. Conversely, people find it stressful to have to act contrary to their values.

A person's values cannot be easily or directly inferred from his personality because values concern a person's private agenda, something he may not always care to share.

I recommend using the MVPI report of Hogan to understand the core values of the person you wish to hire. This gives us a preview of the culture the person will create as a leader through a system of rewards and punishments. Scores between the sixty-sixth and hundredth percentiles are high, while scores between the thirty-fifth and the sixty-fifth percentiles are average. Scores less than the thirty-fourth percentile are low. High scores indicate core business drivers, average scores indicate interests, and low scores do not signify any driver for the person.

'The leader's personalities shape the culture of the organization, team, or business unit. Followers identify and interpret the values implicit in the behaviour and decisions of their leader. Eventually, organizational processes, norms and culture come to resemble the values of the leader.' (Hogan Assessments)

Let us take an example of a leader whose MVPI profile is given here. This report can give you insights that can be used to evaluate the fit between this person and his current occupation. So, with the help of this report one can understand how motivated the leader is in his current role. We shall, however, focus here to see that the report can be used to evaluate the fit between the leader's core values and the corporate culture. No matter how talented the leader might be, if his values are inconsistent with those of the culture, he will rarely succeed in that culture. And finally, certain values enhance and certain other values impede a person's performance as a leader.

MOTIVES, VALUES AND PREFERENCES INVENTORY

The leadership values forecast is based on the MVPI which has ten scales. These are discussed below:

Recognition

A leader who has very high scores on recognition has a desire to be known, seen, be visible and famous. He wants a lifestyle which has opportunities to be noticed and dreams of fame and high achievement, whether or not they are fulfilled.

Power

A leader who is high on power is driven by a desire to succeed, make things happen, make a difference and outperform one's competition.

Hedonism

Leaders with high scores enjoy creating a culture where having fun, excitement and pleasure is valued. They value a lifestyle organized around eating, drinking and entertaining.

Altruistic

Leaders with high scores on this scale have a strong desire to help others, have a concern for the welfare of the less fortunate in life and lead a lifestyle organized around public service and the betterment of humanity.

Affiliation

Leaders with strong scores on affiliation need and enjoy frequent and varied social contact. They like a lifestyle that is organized around social interaction.

Tradition

Leaders with strong scores on this scale have a belief in values such as family, thrift, hard work, appropriate social behaviour. They enjoy a lifestyle that reflects these themes.

Security

Leaders strong on security have a high need for predictability and structure. They will make efforts to avoid risk and uncertainty, especially in the employment area. They enjoy a lifestyle organized around minimizing errors and mistakes.

Commerce

Leaders with high scores on this scale are driven by an interest in earning money, realizing profits, finding new business opportunities. They will follow a lifestyle organized around investments and financial planning.

Aesthetics

Leaders who have high scores on this scale have a high need for self-expression. They care about quality and have an interest in how things look, feel and sound. They pay close attention to the appearance of work products. Design matters to them.

Science

Leaders with high scores in science are highly interested in science, are comfortable with technology and prefer data-based decisions. They are not comfortable with decisions based on intuition or gut feeling. They are always keen to know how things work.

Let us now study the Leadership Values Profile of a leader by analyzing the high scores on the MVPI Profile.

CASE

If you have a leader whose Leadership Values Profile has the following scores, what can we forecast about this person? This leader has high scores of more than sixty-six in all but three of the values.

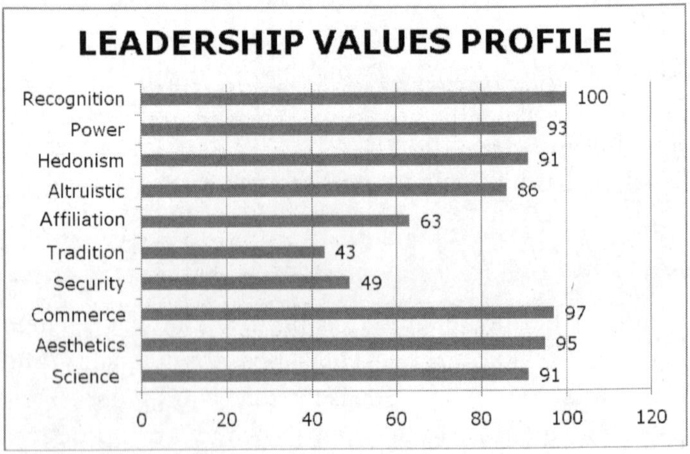

This leader has high scores on recognition, power, hedonism, altruistic, commerce, aesthetics and science. When a person has high scores on several of the scales of MVPI the person will remain unhappy and unfulfilled for some reason or the other. It is equally likely that a person with so many different values will try to find one motive or the other to find satisfaction.

He will enjoy working in a competitive, high-profile role where he can compete against all odds and succeed. He will have a sharp eye for numbers and profits of the enterprise and will make decisions based on data and logic. His reviews with team members will be marked by his seeking answers to questions as he analyses the data reports. High hedonism scores reflect a person who likes to celebrate success with great office parties and off-site meetings where team members will be spoilt for choice about food and celebrations. High power, hedonism and recognition scores will show that when this person celebrates success and victories, he will make a statement. His high need for recognition would mean that he will need frequent feedback and appreciation from his manager. He will stress participation in high-profile projects that will feed this need. His high need for power will mean he would like to take on challenging assignments and will work against all odds to make it succeed. He is going to hate working in an organization where the culture is to distribute rewards uniformly. That would totally demotivate this person. He thrives in a culture of high differentiation. High scores on hedonism would mean he would prefer to work with people who are informal, relaxed and playful and who like to travel and entertain. He will be uncomfortable working in organizations that are formal, bureaucratic and inflexible. Someone with such high scores in commerce would be appreciated by his superiors for his financial drive. While that may be something the organization may like, we also have to keep in mind that the person will value monetary rewards just as much. Such a strong focus on the bottom line may mean that he may forget that success usually depends on the goodwill of others. Since this leader gets motivated by salary increases and financial rewards, he may overlook alternative ways to motivate his team; not everyone is motivated by money.

A person with so many high scores will run the risk of always being unhappy for some reason or the other.

IDEAS

1. At the leadership level, the values of the leader shape the organizational culture very deeply. The MVPI scale tells us about the strong values of the leader better than what even the most skilled interviewer can do by asking questions in an interview. These are deeply held by the individuals and are difficult to uncover and influence. Many new hires makes gaffes that are unpardonable in the culture of the new organization. You should look to understand the mismatch between the individual and the organizational culture. A leader who is very high on aesthetics and hedonism would like to have a nice office. If he works for an organization which will not meet this need, he will always have a niggling irritation at the back of his mind.
2. Values also have an impact on the pride employees feel when they see the values that the company stands for. Congruence between the leader's and the organization's values builds a deep sense of organizational citizenship.
3. Behaviour of the individuals is visible to everyone. Everyone knows what a person is doing through the behaviour. The underlying values tell us *why* the person is doing what he is doing. An insight into the leader's behaviour is a great way to predict the kind of work culture and reward systems the leader will create in the workplace. Alignment of values helps to create an engaged workforce.

12

Values and Organizational Culture

INTRODUCTION

A leader's personality has a very direct impact on the culture of an organization. The simplest way to understand this relation is to look at the rewards and recognition process of an organization. Who is rewarded for what and how can we determine the culture of an organization? Are promotions announced and celebrated? What are the organization's policies around employee compensation and travel? If you dig deeper, you will often see the organization mirroring the values of the most influential leader of the organization. If the values of the new hire do not have a strong fit, sooner or later the person will leave the organization. Worse still, if the person does not leave, he will be a huge drag on the morale.

Alan Lewis says:

> Employees who do not adhere to a shared corporate culture dilute it, detracting from the essence that gives your company its identity and helps it achieve aggressive

> goals. In my view, every organization's hiring process—from Microsoft to PS 90 to everything in between—should screen candidates for the best cultural fit. *(How My Company Hires for Culture First, Skills Second, 2011)*

CULTURE DEFINED

My favourite definition is that organizational culture is 'the way things get done around here' (Deal & Kennedy, 1982). An organization's culture is a complex collection of unspoken norms of behaviour that govern any organization. Culture is made up of the values, beliefs, underlying assumptions, attitudes and behaviours shared by a group of people. Culture is the behaviour that results when a group arrives at a set of generally unspoken and unwritten rules for working together. According to research this has significance for organizations that seek to attract high quality applicants. (Catanzaro, Moore & Marshall, 2010)

The role of the leader in shaping the organization's culture is easy to imagine. So organizations need to seriously consider the fit between the current or desired organizational culture and CEO characteristics. Organizations attempting to change fundamental aspects of its functioning may need significant behavioural changes at the top (Giberson, Resick, Dickson, Mitchelson & Randall, 2009).

Culture is the single most important factor accounting for success or failure in organizations. For the sake of simplicity, if we assume that the values of the leader shapes the policies and the culture, a leader who is strongly motivated by the value of commerce will create rewards that are more financially lucrative. We often tend to assume that what motivates us also is valued by others. So if the organization is driven by commerce, the opportunity to motivate people through non-financial incentives will not be easily seen.

Let us examine the following case to understand how the organizational values impact the dominant strands of its culture.

CASE

In 2006–07, India's general insurance market witnessed a variety of changes. On the whole, the sector achieved double-digit growth and this trend is expected to persist over the medium term. According to the erstwhile Investment and Credit Rating Agency ICRA, the 281-billion-rupee Indian general insurance industry reported a compounded annual growth rate (CAGR) of 15.1 per cent over the last five years. The ICRA report on Indian general insurance industry says that currently, there are fourteen active general insurance companies in the country, including four from the public sector. Over the last five years, the private sector entities have reported strong growth and together they now have a market share of around 60 per cent. While the public sector players remain the largest in the industry, the gap between the top three private sector players and the public sector entities has narrowed substantially during the last few years. Overall, the top eight players in the Indian general insurance industry continue to account for over 90 per cent of the total business.

MaximumCover Insurance is a well-known player in the non-life-insurance business worldwide. Their Indian operation has been growing at a steady pace. But over the last three years they have been falling behind their peers. With a change of the

> CEO, MaximumCover veterans say that the entire culture has undergone a change. There is no respect for tenure and long service but underperforming employees have been asked to go rather unceremoniously. In the past they would have been given some 'special projects' and accommodated in some customized role within the organization. The sales team was given stretch targets that the new CEO would review on a weekly basis. The new CEO made it a point to meet customers every week and told everyone that senior leaders' performance bonus would depend on significantly improving customer satisfaction. Analysts say that the new CEO Roy is doing everything to make MaximumCover win in the marketplace but everyone agrees it is not the same any more.

The organization is reconciling to the whole idea of job security. From an erstwhile paternalistic culture where poor performers continued to coexist with high performers, the CEO is trying to promote a culture where high performers are valued. Under performers are unceremoniously dumped regardless of their previous tenure. One may argue that the economic scenario or the competitive landscape is driving this behaviour. Yet, there is no doubt that the employees who will succeed and be happy in the new culture would be of a different mental make up from the long tenured.

ELEMENTS OF ORGANIZATIONAL CULTURE

The values of the leaders get reflected in the organization. We have looked at the MVPI as a framework that can help us understand values at an individual level. We will use the same framework to understand different elements of the culture that get influenced by the values of the leader. While the scores have been articulated in two extremes, high or low, you may recognize shades of the extremes in different parts of the same organization. This apparent contradiction can be traced back to the influence of different leaders at different times as the organization has evolved.

The different processes of the organizational culture that can be influenced by the values of the leader are discussed below:

Recognition

An organization that has a high recognition culture will be very active in managing the media. The leaders are expected to be known, seen, visible and famous. Tasks, if completed successfully, will be noticed and applauded. You may expect such organizations to take part in all the surveys that magazines run among companies and splash it everywhere once they feature at the top in some listing. The leaders are expected to take on the competitors openly and head-on even in public forums. An organization that is high on recognition values networking and external relationships. The leaders are encouraged to take up leadership roles in various industry forums.

The companies which are low on recognition will be shy of the media. The prevailing philosophy is: 'If you are good, others will get to know it. Don't blow your own trumpet.' Such organizations believe that competition does not lie outside, but within. Networking and participation in industry bodies are looked upon as a waste of time. In such companies the reward and recognition programmes are understated and private. Promotions are often not announced across the organization. Newly promoted leaders have to underplay their achievements because celebratory parties are not encouraged. The focus is on maintaining harmonious relationships by not highlighting differences between individual performances and results. Rewards are almost always private and low-key. When people miss targets they are given another chance to work on something they are likely to succeed in.

Power

An organization that is high on power in their culture is driven by a desire to succeed, make things happen, make a difference and outperform competition. The leaders are encouraged to aggressively pursue opportunities to increase the profitability of the business. Employees are expected to take up challenging assignments. The organizational vision too emphasizes achievement of results and the rewards are skewed in favour of people who produce them. The organization is alive to the external environment and the changes in the competitive landscape form a part of regular meetings of the leaders. Sales conferences are often marked by chest-thumping declarations of 'decimating competition'. In one company I saw the CEO take the competitor's logo (printed on a large sheet of paper) and put it into an oversized paper-shredder at the end of a dramatic speech that stressed on absolute dominance in the heart of the consumer. In cultures that are high on power, the stress is on driving projects to completion. Individual achievement is celebrated even when teamwork takes a beating. The joke in such organizations is that they spend as much time plotting internal showdowns as they do with competitors.

Organizations that are low on power emphasize consensus and cooperation, rather than competition and challenge. Leaders are expected to avoid pushing their staff. They believe that it is better when people can work at their own pace, get things done without supervision and choose work processes they desire. Organizations that are low on power tend to operate on a laissez-faire approach. The guidelines from the corporate office or headquarters are taken as a suggestion, not a mandate. Aggressive employees are disliked. Assertive leaders are equally disliked. Because of this approach, leaders may not provide a clear vision that they want the organization to achieve. The organization dislikes leaders who achieve results but demotivate the team by micromanaging. Trust, respect and support are valued more than having lots of opportunities for upward career mobility. The belief is that the market is large enough to accommodate many players and they just need to find their own niche.

Hedonism

Organizations with high scores on hedonism have a culture where having fun, excitement and pleasure is valued. Eating, drinking and entertaining are important elements of this culture. When leaders travel to remote locations and branch offices, they will be encouraged to spend their evenings meeting employees informally. These are informal meetings and are marked by humour, bonhomie and laughter. Leaders ensure that they keep things interesting. It is a 'work hard, play hard' culture. The workplace offers plenty of occasions where employees can play, entertain, amuse others and have opportunities to have a good time. Leaders create opportunities for staff to unwind and to have fun, as a way of motivating them. The work environment promotes expression and spontaneity. In some organizations, the all-employees meetings are marked by skits where junior employees take digs at senior leaders without fear of retaliation. The organization's culture is best described as informal and relaxed. The leaders take pride in having an open-door policy and are seen to be approachable.

Organizations which are low on hedonism value a serious, business-like attitude in the workplace and frown upon employees who are not so task-oriented. Rules and formal procedures are encouraged. Exceptions are seen to be a sign of weakness. A leader is expected to set the example of adhering to the rules. Employees will like the predictability of such a culture, but may find such an 'all-business' attitude wearisome, if it persists over time. There is low value placed on social functions at work, but are sometimes justified as a way of keeping the staff morale high and increasing productivity. Adherence to office timings and dress codes characterize a low hedonistic culture. These cultures tend to frown upon expenses on entertainment and having fun. The workplace is hierarchical and emphasizes discipline and clear focus on job-related issues. People are often looked at as a factor of production just like land or machinery. The office atmosphere is formal. Their functional offices remind employees to put business before pleasure.

Altruistic

Organizations with high altruistic scores display a strong desire to help others. Their corporate social responsibility programmes are well-structured and the senior leaders are expected to drive those initiatives with equal gusto. Such cultures encourage their employees to have a concern for the welfare of the less fortunate in life and lead a lifestyle organized around public service and the betterment of humanity. These organizations may slip up on holding people accountable for their performance. Second, some employees, vendors and other stakeholders may try to take advantage of this behaviour. For example, employees will soon discover that talking about the challenges in their personal life will often get them off the hook for missing performance targets. Junior employees will expect the leader to take an active interest on issues of staff morale and to advocate for their needs. Altruistic cultures create team commitment by working hard to please employees through creative initiatives that draw on the staff welfare fund. A culture high on altruism encourages co-workers to assist one another. Leaders are expected to actively improve employee morale in addition to accomplishment and results. They encourage volunteering and giving back to the community and have policies that give paid time-off for employees if they take up a community-related initiative. The leaders are generous in offering staff flexibility when dealing with personal problems. Selfish people are seen to be outcasts in this culture.

Organizations that score low on the altruistic scale encourage their leaders to be direct and outspoken and confront people-related problems. They tend to pay more attention to the interests of the organization than the individuals who make it up. The leader's prime task is to be task-oriented. The culture promotes business issues over morale. Employees are expected to deal with their personal problems without letting the office know about it. These cultures work on the belief that flexi time and work from home are new-fangled ways that lower accountability. They view the relationship between employer and employee to be like a business contract with no room for emotions.

Affiliation

Organizations with a strong affiliation culture have an almost compulsive need for frequent and varied social interaction. The unofficial and official processes are designed to maximize social contact. The long weekly meetings of the leadership team blend in work and socialization. A new person joining or leaving the team is a good enough reason to socialize and have fun. The relationships built during informal interactions impact the effectiveness with which a person operates in the office. After-office parties and celebrations are frequent and missing them can completely alienate a leader. Besides an overdose of scheduled meetings there will be plenty of spontaneous meetings that involve several people but often result in no decisions being taken. The office design encourages interaction. The heroes of the office will be those who are popular and the loners are outcasts. Leaders are expected to be outgoing, articulate and energetic. The popular leaders tend to be socially adaptable and spontaneous. The culture encourages problem solving between units through face-to-face meetings over meals and possibly an after-office party.

Organizations that are low on affiliation value the need for individual privacy and recognize the employees' need for private time. Giving spontaneous feedback to a colleague is rare. Relationships at work are with a few close colleagues. The leaders rarely eat lunch with anyone else. Leaders may have very few friends at work and most of them like to work independently. Working in teams or taking decisions by encouraging dialogue with the rest of the organization is a challenge. The culture does not place a high value on socializing with colleagues. The dominant mode of communication is email. Colleagues sitting in adjoining cubicles at work may prefer communicating through electronic chat rooms or social media. Decisions are often taken between a few people and then communicated to the rest of the organization via email or a memo. Meetings are seen to be a distraction. The emphasis is on being productive rather than getting everyone's participation and opinion. These organizations respect individual contributions over team activities. They value enhancing existing relationships over developing new networks.

Tradition

Organizations that are strong on tradition take pride in their past and make it a point to tell everyone about it. The culture places a lot of value on history, family ties and has clear standards of what is acceptable as norms of interacting with colleagues within and outside of the workplace. These organizations are conservative in nature. Leaders are expected to uphold these values and live according to them even in their personal lifestyle.

A culture that is high on tradition will be typified by clear dress codes and grooming standards, clear hierarchy and reporting structure. It is not unusual to have codified rules about decorating desks and workspaces. There will be rituals that glorify patriotism, and the pictures of senior government officials like the president or the prime minister (and certainly of the founder) will be prominently displayed in office. Museums and libraries will showcase documents and correspondence of prominent leaders of the past. The senior leaders will be the likely heroes. These cultures value predictability in the work environment. Conformity is expected. Some family-owned businesses, factories and organizations where business is highly routinized and process driven tend to thrive in values of high tradition. They expect leaders to be somewhat cautious, and they deliberate hard before making choices. They resist change.

Organizations that have weak scores on tradition tend to value liberal ideas, are flexible and encourage unconventional environments. Organizations in sunrise industries often tend to have these cultures. Organizations that deal with creative arts, for example, media and advertising agencies, tend to have cultures that are low in tradition. They tend to be much more flexible about what is acceptable as a dress code at work. The employees are free to wear casual, informal clothes to work. Their tattoos and piercings are accepted as part of their individuality. Such organizations encourage these expressions. The employees' personal lives also reflect this acceptance. So, living together, frequent changing of partners, divorces, etc., do not raise any eyebrows. There is no discrimination among employees because of disability or sexual preferences. They state that they are equal opportunity employers. Unconventional behaviour is expected of leaders. Anything that has shock value is glorified in the culture of low tradition. They embrace and thrive on change.

Security

Organizational cultures that are strong on security have a high need for predictability and structure. They will make efforts to avoid risk and uncertainty. Errors are frowned upon. These are strong 'Plan B' cultures. The leaders spend their time worrying about errors, leaks and mistakes and keep designing processes that are a guard against real or imagined eventualities. These include security procedures, frequent fire drills, disaster recovery procedures and a strong culture that rewards compliance in order to minimize risks. The leaders are not expected to make mistakes; they are expected to prevent others from making mistakes. Every error in judgement is looked upon as a total failure of the leader. This is a risk-averse culture that encourages people to double-check all plans and ensure that no loophole has been left unplugged. The culture tends to encourage high-quality, low-risk decisions. Entry into new markets or trying out untested solutions is hard for these organizations. Impatient leaders are frowned upon. Perfection is appreciated even if it takes time.

Organizational cultures that are low on security are marked by the freedom they give to employees to take chances, test limits and make quick changes. The leaders are expected to try out an idea even when it is not fully thought through. It is better that leaders test-drive an idea that is still considered work in progress than to wait until the idea is foolproof. Speed of implementation is valued more than perfection. The risk appetite in such an organization is high. People are not afraid to try out an idea, no matter how unconventional it is. The reward and recognition system of these organizations is designed to encourage innovation. Leaders in these cultures are expected to be outgoing, adventurous and assertive. The tolerance for ambiguity is high. Their policies and procedures are ever evolving and sometimes not even updated for a long time because the 'employees look at the rules as guidelines'. The leaders are expected to have a high appetite for accepting criticism. Companies which are known to bring in path-breaking and iconic products or trendsetters in any field are usually low on tradition.

Commerce

Organizational cultures that are strong on commerce emphasize profitability and cost containment. People who raise money, develop business or devise clever ideas that help to bring down the costs of operation are heroes of these cultures. The leaders look at all the decisions by the impact on the bottom line. The finance department and sales functions are relatively more powerful as they tend to have a say in many decisions taken by other functions. The rewards in the organizations are all financial incentives and hence in a year when margins are under pressure, the leaders feel helpless in motivating the employees.

Financial analysis and cost-benefit analysis are ongoing processes based on which decisions are evaluated. The leaders who do well in such environments are people who are ambitious, hard-working and practical. They monitor budgets and display cost consciousness. They value material success and money for the business as well as for themselves. The culture of organizations high on commerce tends to be well planned, organized and mature. Money, fame and success are valued. When senior leaders get together, the talk seems to revolve around profits, money, stock market tips, etc.

Organizational cultures that are weak on commerce often miss out on evaluating the financial aspect of the decision. They may take on clients because the 'assignment seemed challenging and interesting' even when it did not make money for the company. The leaders in these cultures are expected to value relationships over profitability. They value good ideas, intellectual challenge and having fun as important drivers in the workplace. The leaders are often liked but find it hard to drive people for results. When the leaders meet socially, the conversation is rarely about how to make money or about the lifestyles of the rich. Financial discipline is missing and it is common to discover cost overruns at the end of the year. The human element is far more important than its financial implication. These leaders struggle to take decisions on layoffs or staff reduction and will try to compensate the affected people with severance packages that are very generous and much more than industry norms. Leaders in such cultures believe that there is more to life than chasing quarterly profit targets to please analysts. They are described as friendly and generous by the employees.

Aesthetics

Organizations that are high on aesthetics have a high need for self-expression. A conscious effort is made to make the offices look unique in terms of style, appearance, quality or 'good taste'. Appearances matter. The furniture, the rugs, the paintings and lighting in the office will be expensive, subtle and understated. Even the coffee cups and office stationery will be elegantly designed and reflect good taste. Comfort and leisure of employees are valued and every effort is made so that they operate in an ergonomic setting that is well designed. Some luxury hotels are synonymous with high aesthetics, not just for the guest rooms but for the quality of the staff cafeteria. They care about quality and have an interest in how things look, feel and sound. They pay close attention to the appearance of work products. Design matters to them. To know where the organization stands on the continuum from low to high on aesthetics, look at the travel policies, the quality of fittings and furniture in the offices and the quality of the food and crockery used in the cafeteria. The heroes in such a culture will be known for their etiquette and fine taste. Innovation and a freethinking attitude are parts of this culture.

Organizations that are low on aesthetics use functionality and cost as key drivers (if the organization is also high on commerce). Style and design are viewed to be a waste. The workplace furniture and fittings will be spartan. The cafeteria will focus on standards that are 'good enough'. The work culture of organizations low on aesthetics tends to value leaders who are stable, predictable and dependable. Emotions are kept under control in the workplace. Leaders will reward people for persisting with boring tasks, and problems are solved in practical, never innovative ways. Issues of personal autonomy are not important and the appearance of work products does not feature in the leaders' concerns. Any policy that impacts leisure or comfort of the employee is viewed from pure functionality and is kept at just above the threshold of frugality. Longevity of the furniture and fittings is more important than how it looks. Leaders who are seen to worry about design and 'finish' are often suspected of not being good enough in their work. Style is viewed as a cheap substitute for substance. Leaders in such cultures value practical problem solving and running things by the rule book rather than innovation. Output is measured in quantity rather than quality. The organization will resist innovative ideas as being 'impractical and difficult to implement'. Experimentation is hard in such a culture.

Science

Organization cultures that are high in science are highly interested in and comfortable with technology and prefer data-based decisions. There is an emphasis on the rigour and defensibility of the plans, goals and decisions and public statements. Anyone's views can be challenged and the person is expected to defend his position. Decisions based on intuition or gut feeling come in for criticism. Policies and procedures are based on evidence and rationality. Analytics rule supreme in this culture. Review meetings with the CEO or senior leaders are marked by rigorous questioning of data, methodology and conclusions. An employee will go in for the review armed with mountains of data and supporting evidence not knowing what will come in handy to stave off the attack. Conversely, during all-employee meetings, employees will often punch holes in the logic of the policies and if proved right, the leader will be expected to reverse the decision. The nerds and geeks are the heroes of this culture. Leaders will be expected to be logical, disciplined and rigorous and to be able to make data-based decisions. Cultures that are high in science value problem-solving environments. Curiosity and analytical problem-solving followed by objective decision making are the norm. The leaders are expected to be tech-savvy and quick to integrate new technology on an ongoing basis. Data are treated as a means to identify trends. Leaders in these cultures are very smart people who lack leadership skills. They are easily bored, argumentative, easily annoyed and prefer analysis to action. Being labelled an 'airhead' can be the worst thing that happens to an employee in such a culture.

Organizational cultures that score low on science are uninterested in science and technology. They are more comfortable working with people than technology. So the IT system of these organizations is often patchy and outdated. Leaders in these environments are comfortable with intuition and gut feeling in making decisions. Data are used as a support or influence mechanism. Leaders prefer a spontaneous rather than planned and systematic approach to problem solving. They have a bias for action rather than analysis. They tend to be sympathetic, open to feedback and responsive to criticism. Their team members will often describe them as responsible, flexible and willing to make mistakes. Leaders create a culture that value doing things 'well enough' rather than being well grounded in data and analysis.

You can get a snapshot of your company culture by rating your company from low to high on all MVPI dimensions. Ask your colleagues to do the same. That should give you a good idea about your culture.

IDEAS

1. The organizational cultures have been described along ten scales as being high or low. On each of these ten scales, the culture will be somewhere along a continuum. It is the combination of these elements that makes culture come alive.
2. The leader influences the culture very sharply based on his values. Understanding the different scales can greatly help the leader to understand what levers to use in accomplishing his mandate. Everything from the design of the rewards and recognition policies, travel and leisure policies, how junior employees will behave towards him, etc., can be viewed through the lens of culture.
3. When the leader understands his own values and the impact he has on risk taking, decision making and on the culture of innovation in the firm, he can always counterbalance his own style by working with another senior leader whose style has elements that the organization is trying to build in to succeed in a fluid business environment.

13

Conclusion

Hiring right requires an approach that is different from hiring 'the best'. Here is a recap of the steps.

Step 1

The first step is to understand the demands of the role for which we are hiring. To do this, create a Success Profile^{SM} for the role. This should tell you not just the qualifications and experience needed for the role, but you should also do the stakeholder analysis to identify the competencies that will be needed for the role. Lastly, identify the enablers and derailers in the personality of the candidate. It helps if we also plot the culture of the organization where the person will operate.

Step 2

Use the Hogan Personality Inventory to assess the 'bright side' of personality. This is what others will observe in the candidate when they work with him on a day-to-day basis. This also tells us whether the person has the personality elements that enable him to do what the role demands. For example, in a sales job, you need someone who is outgoing, takes risks and enjoys influencing. In an air traffic controller's job you need someone with steady nerves. You don't want someone with his personality in a sales role.

Step 3

Use the Hogan Development Survey to identify the personality derailers or the 'dark side' of the personality. These derailers will warn you about potential issues that may come up. A strength that is overused becomes a derailer. Find out what derailers are in the high-risk zone. These are derailers that show up when a person is not actively managing his public image. For example, derailers can stop someone from taking quick decisions. Excitable people will have mood swings when under stress, etc. Assessment of personality can help you take an informed decision ahead of time. So the organization can put support systems in place that will help the leader succeed. That could be in the form of a coach or in the form of a team that complements. The bright and dark side can predict how much the person will enjoy doing the job that is being offered.

Step 4

Assess the motivation of the individual. This helps to find a fit with the organization's culture and the leader. In the absence of a strong fit between the leader's and the organization's values, you can expect low engagement and, more likely, the leader to leave at the earliest opportunity. A fit with the organization's culture builds employee engagement and organizational citizenship.

Step 5

Hiring right is when the person matches the demands of the role, is motivated to do it and can be himself in the context of the organizational culture fit. Whether you are an entrepreneur who is seeking to hire one additional leader for a twenty-employee organization or you are hiring a few leaders for the top team of a global corporation with thousands of employees, you can follow this process. The cost of following this process is negligible compared to the cost of a wrong hire. So at the leadership level, do not hire the best!

Bibliography

Amabile, T. and S. Kramer. *Talent, Passion, and the Creativity Maze.* http://blogs.hbr.org; http://blogs.hbr.org/hbsfaculty/2012/02/talent-passion-and-the-creativ.html (accessed 27 February 2012).

Anders, G. *The Rare Find: Spotting Exceptional Talent Before Everyone Else.* Portfolio, 2011.

Bhaduri, A. *Interview: George Anders.* http://abhijitbhaduri.com; http://abhijitbhaduri.com/2012/06/interview-george-anders/ (accessed 23 June 2012).

Bryant, A. *The Corner Office.* New York: Henry Holt and Co., 2011.

Catanzaro, D., H. Moore and T. Marshall. 'The impact of organizational culture on attraction and recruitment of job applicants', *Journal of Business and Psychology.* 2010.

Deal, T. and A. Kennedy. *Corporate Cultures: The Rites and Rituals of Corporate Life.* Harmondsworth: Penguin, 1982.

Favaro, K., P. O. Karlsson and G.L. Neilson. *Strategy and Business.* http://www.strategy-business.com/article/12207?gko=00863 (accessed 24 May 2012).

Giberson, T., C. Resick, M. Dickson, J. Mitchelson and K. Randall. 'Leadership and Organizational Culture: Linking

CEO Characteristics to Cultural Values', *Journal of Business and Psychology*, 2009, pp. 123–137.

Gilbert, D. *Stumbling on Happiness*. New York: Alfred A. Knopf, 2006.

Glassdoor. *Top 25 Oddball Interview Questions of 2011*. http://www.glassdoor.com/blog/top-25-oddball-interview-questions-2011/ (accessed 28 December 2011).

Harrison, D.A. 'How Important are Job Attitudes?' *Academy of Management Journal* 49, no. 2, 2006, pp. 320–321.

Hogan Assessments. *The Culture Clash–Hogan Assessment Systems*. http://www.hoganassessments.nl; http://www.hoganassessments. nl/uploads/file/Whitepapers/Culture%20Clash_R2.pdf

Hogan, R. and R. Warrenfeltz. 'Educating the Modern Manager', *Academy of Management Learning and Education* 2, no. 1, 2003, pp. 74–84.

How My Company Hires for Culture First, Skills Second. http://blogs.hbr.org/cs/2011/01/how_my_company_hires_ for_cultu.html (accessed 26 January 2011).

Inc Magazine. *The 4 Hiring Practices of Highly Successful Organizations*. http://www.inc.com/articles/2002/01/23815.html

Lee, J. *How To Land A Job In Another Industry*. http://www.forbes.com/2010/09/28/how-to-get-jobs-in-another-industry-entrepreneurs-human-resources-sustainable-tech-10.html (accessed 28 September 2010).

Perina, K., C. Flora and H.E. Marano. *Who Are You? (And What do You Think of Me?)*. http://www.psychologytoday.com/articles/201012/who-are-you-and-what-do-you-think-me (accessed 11 January 2012).

Acknowledgements

We learn in strange ways. I realized this in the process of writing this book. Snatches of conversations, books, listening to practitioners and meandering discussions with friends and colleagues have built my understanding of how to hire the right person for the right job. Then over the last four years I have researched this topic consciously to understand why it is so hard to get this right. In a world that chases labels, it is hard not to want to hire the best. At senior levels that can be a recipe for disaster.

This outline of the book started after exchanging several emails with Claudio Fernández-Aráoz of the search firm Egon Zehnder and author of *Great People Decisions*. *Businessweek* magazine named him one of the world's most influential headhunters. When I read his book, I thought there is very little left to write on the subject. Claudio helped me carve out this unexplored territory. Sonny Iqbal (Egon Zehnder)—thanks for introducing me to Claudio and for your wisdom.

I have been lucky to be able to exchange ideas and

learn from many friends. You will see that they represent firms that are global benchmarks.

You may not realize how our conversations have influenced this book. I know that for sure. So thank you V.R. Ferose (SAP Labs), Rajan Anandan and Sunil Malik (Google), Smita Affinwalla (DDI), Navnit Singh (Korn Ferry), Mohinish Sinha (The Hay Group), Rajiv Krishnan (Mercer), Arun Das Mahapatra (Heidrick and Struggles), Atanu Basu (Ayata), Krish Shankar (Bharti Airtel), SY Siddiqui (Maruti Suzuki) and Gautam Ghosh (social media expert) and to my professors at XLRI who taught me so many things, which I have only begun to understand now (yes, I am slow). Thanks to my erstwhile colleagues at PepsiCo, Microsoft, Colgate, Mudra, Tata Steel and Eicher for giving me a chance to understand the nuances of hiring.

Chapal Mehra, Vijay Nair and Anand S (Suspi) and to colleagues at Wipro, thank you for reading some of the early drafts of the book and helping me bring focus and structure to my writing.

Thanks to DDI and the Hay Group for letting me use their frameworks and refer to their research in my book. I got certified as a Hogan Coach many years back. I believe it is the most comprehensive framework one can use to assess leaders for fit with the role and the organization's culture. Thanks to Dr Robert Hogan for letting me use the framework and giving me access to years of research on personality. The base of the book lies in the framework developed by Dr Robert Hogan.

Karthika, Sukumar, Shantanu, Shuka and the team at HarperCollins—thanks for making the book happen. Finally!

Notes

Notes

Notes